From Your Friends At **The MAILBOX®**

APRIL

A MONTH OF REPRODUCIBLES AT YOUR FINGERTIPS!

Y0-CZN-321

Grades 4–5

Senior Editor:
Thad H. McLaurin

Writers:
Rusty Fischer, Elizabeth H. Lindsay, Debra Liverman,
Thad H. McLaurin, Cindy Mondello, Patricia Twohey

Art Coordinator:
Clevell Harris

Artists:
Cathy Spangler Bruce, Pam Crane,
Nick Greenwood, Clevell Harris, Sheila Krill,
Mary Lester, Rob Mayworth, Kimberly Richard

Cover Artist:
Jennifer Tipton Bennett

www.themailbox.com

©1998 by THE EDUCATION CENTER, INC.
All rights reserved.
ISBN #1-56234-219-3

Manufactured in the United States

10 9 8 7 6 5 4 3 2

Table Of Contents

April Calendar 3
Activities for free-time fun.

Events And Activities For The Family 4
Three events and activities for parents and students to explore at home.

Mathematics Education Month 5
Celebrate a month of math with these challenging reproducibles.

National Garden Month 13
Let these exciting activities help you plant the seeds of knowledge in your students' minds.

National Humor Month 17
Rid your class of the blues with these rib-tickling activities.

National Poetry Month 21
Roses are red. Violets are blue. These poetry activities are perfect for you!

National School Library Month 27
Help your students learn more about your school's library with these reproducible activities.

National Reading A Road Map Day 33
Chart your course for National Reading A Road Map Day with an assortment of map-skill activities and reproducibles.

National Week Of The Ocean 37
Explore the wonders of the ocean with these reproducible activities.

Astronomy Week 41
Blast off with these creative activities that will send your study of astronomy into orbit!

Thomas Jefferson's Birthday 45
Use these reproducibles to help your students learn more about this man of many talents.

National Coin Week 49
Put your money where your mouth is with these fun coin-related reproducibles.

Earth Day 53
Help keep America beautiful with these Earth-smart activities.

Arbor Day 59
You'll have it made in the shade with these tree-loving activities.

Answer Keys 63

April Calendar: free-time activities

April Free Time

MONDAY	TUESDAY	WEDNESDAY	THURSDAY	FRIDAY
April 1 is April Fools' Day. What is a practical joke? Why do people play them? 	National Automobile Month is in April. Write a paragraph about what life would be like without automobiles.	On April 3, 1860, the Pony Express began its route between Missouri and California. Explain how the Pony Express is different from our modern mail system. Then tell the ways in which it is similar. 	Write a limerick about spring. 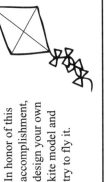	Public Schools Week is in April. List three things you like about your school. List one improvement you would make.
Mathematics Education Month is observed during the month of April. In recognition of this event, write three word problems and challenge a classmate to complete them. $+, \times, \div, -$	April is Keep America Beautiful Month. List five ways you and your classmates can make the world a more beautiful place. Fill Me Up With Trash!	National Library Week is celebrated in April. In honor of this occasion, make a list of your favorite books; then share the list with a friend.	In 1976, Kazukiko Asaba flew 1,050 kites at the same time. In honor of this accomplishment, design your own kite model and try to fly it. 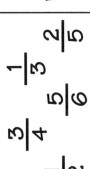	April is National Youth Sports Safety Month. List five safety rules you and your classmates should follow when participating in a sport. 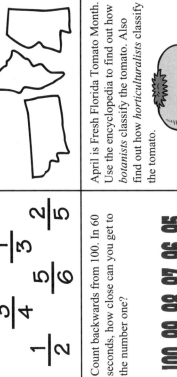
Draw a road map showing how to get from your house to your school. Road map to school	On April 13, 1796, the first elephant arrived in America. On what continents are elephants found in the wild?	List ten words that rhyme with *spring*. Spring 1. fling 2. 3. 4. 5. 6. 7. 8. 9. 10.	Explain the difference between a *numerator* and a *denominator*. $$\frac{1}{2} \quad \frac{3}{4} \quad \frac{5}{6} \quad \frac{1}{3} \quad \frac{2}{5}$$	Name as many states as you can that begin with the letter *M*.
Use the words *seen* and *scene* correctly in the same sentence.  Scene 1 Take 2	Make as many words as you can from the letters in the word *recyclable*. RECYCLABLE	Make a brochure illustrating different items that can be recycled. Paper • Aluminum • Plastic	Count backwards from 100. In 60 seconds, how close can you get to the number one? 100, 99, 98, 97, 96, 95, ...	April is Fresh Florida Tomato Month. Use the encyclopedia to find out how *botanists* classify the tomato. Also find out how *horticulturalists* classify the tomato. 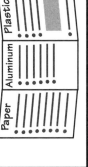

Note To The Teacher: Have each student staple a copy of this page in a file folder. Direct students to store their completed work inside their folders.

3

APRIL
Events And Activities For The Family

Directions: Select at least one activity below to complete as a family by the end of February. *(Challenge: See if your family can complete all three activities.)*

National Reading A Road Map!

In recognition of National Reading A Road Map Week (observed annually from April 4–10), take your family on a make-believe road adventure. Purchase an inexpensive road map of a specific U.S. region. Use the map to plan out the itinerary for an imaginary vacation. On a piece of poster board, record your planned route—highways, interstates, and roads—as well as any stops for sightseeing, meals, and lodging. Present your dream vacation to the rest of the class pointing out key locations on the road map as you do so.

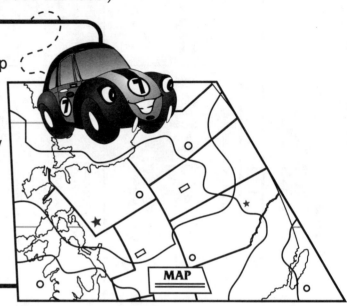

MAP

Penny-Pinchers

On April 16th, 1988, the residents of Fort Madison, Iowa, raised $12,383.06 in pennies for a playground. The residents housed their 1,238,306 pennies in the high school gymnasium. To get a sense of Fort Madison's accomplishment, cover a dollar bill with 100 pennies. Then estimate how many dollar bills would be needed to cover your kitchen or dining room table. Next, trace a dollar bill on drawing paper and cut out enough to cover your kitchen or dining room table. Now calculate how many kitchen tables could be covered with $12,383.06.

Bev's Birthday Bash

Beverly Cleary, the famous children's book author, was born on April 12, 1916. She is well known for her series of *Ramona* books as well as for *Strider* and *The Mouse And The Motorcycle.* In honor of Beverly Cleary's birthday as well as to celebrate National Library Month, select one of Cleary's books to read aloud to your family. Listed at the right are some of Cleary's best-known books.

The Mouse And The Motorcycle
Muggie Maggie
Ramona And Her Father
Ramona And Her Mother
Ramona Quimby, Age 8
Runaway Ralph
Socks
Strider

Note To The Teacher: Distribute one copy of this page to each student at the beginning of the month. Encourage each family to complete at least one activity by the end of April.

4

Mathematics Education Month is observed each year during the month of April and is sponsored by the National Council Of Teachers Of Mathematics.

Everyday Math

Pair your students; then have each pair peruse a grocery-store flyer to plan a party for five friends. Explain that each pair has a total of $30 to spend on anything in the store flyer. Instruct each pair to create a store receipt to show what it purchased and the cost of its total bill. Have the students determine which group got the most for its money.

What Number Am I?

Write the riddle below on the chalkboard. Then challenge your students to find at least five different answers to the riddle.

I am an even number. My ones digit is less than my tens digit. I am less than 100 but greater than 1. List the numbers. (Possible answers: 10, 32, 54, 76, 98.)

Estimation Fun

Use this simple activity to help your students brush up on their estimation skills. Divide your students into small groups. Give each group one individual-size bag of M&M's® candies, a pencil, and a sheet of paper. Instruct each group to estimate the number of M&M's® in its bag and record its guess on the sheet of paper. Then have each group open its bag and count the exact number of candies found in its bag. Instruct each group to record the exact number on its sheet of paper. Identify any groups whose estimates and exact numbers are the same; then have each group tell the rest of the class the exact number of M&M's® candies found in its bag. Have the students determine the average number of candies found in a bag based on this data. Extend the activity by having each group repeat the activity with a bag of peanut M&M's®. Then have students compare the data to see which bag of M&M's® contains more candy. End the activity by letting your students sample the tasty treats.

EQUATION SEARCH

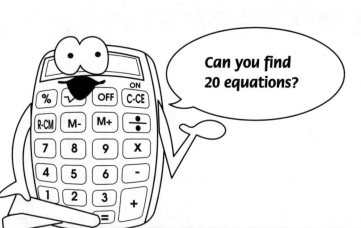

Can you find 20 equations?

Directions: Find three connected numerals that make a true addition or subtraction equation. Each set of three numbers must be in a straight row, column, or diagonal.

76	52	24	62	115	98	23	13	10
19	22	89	73	20	93	14	7	92
95	47	126	82	135	31	80	90	102
33	70	17	73	41	27	52	22	87
56	130	22	58	53	33	92	69	58
15	13	105	10	57	20	72	25	61
110	19	43	78	87	89	33	49	100
44	69	14	13	43	56	12	36	85
66	55	11	99	44	23	8	7	15

Bonus Box: Create a multiplication and division equation search on the back of this sheet. Exchange papers with a friend and see who can be the first to solve the other's equation search.

Name _____

Multiplication Workout

Welcome to Mr. Calculator's P.E. class! Mr. C (as his students affectionately call him) begins each class with heart-thumping, blood-rushing exercises. As a student in Mr. C's class, you must complete the stair-stepping drill.

Directions: Fill in the boxes on the steps by solving the problems in the Across box. Show your work on another sheet of paper. Then follow the directions in the Bonus Box at the bottom of the page.

Across
A. 35 x 33
B. 73 x 69
C. 99 x 64
D. 123 x 24
E. 523 x 42
F. 3,213 x 29
G. 125 x 45
H. 929 x 91
I. 95 x 93

Down
J. 3 x 5
K. 2 x 253
L. 86 x 62
M. 88 x 84
N. 31 x 21
O. 23 x 13
P. 7 x 9
Q. 15 x 41
R. 32 x 24
S. 453 x 16
T. 31 x 18
U. 11 x 3
V. 19 x 5

Bonus Box: Check your work by solving the problems in the Down box.

Name _____

"A-MAZE-ING" MULTIPLICATION

Directions: To complete the maze, first find each product. Then search for a trail of even products beginning at "Start" and ending at the correct "Finish."

START

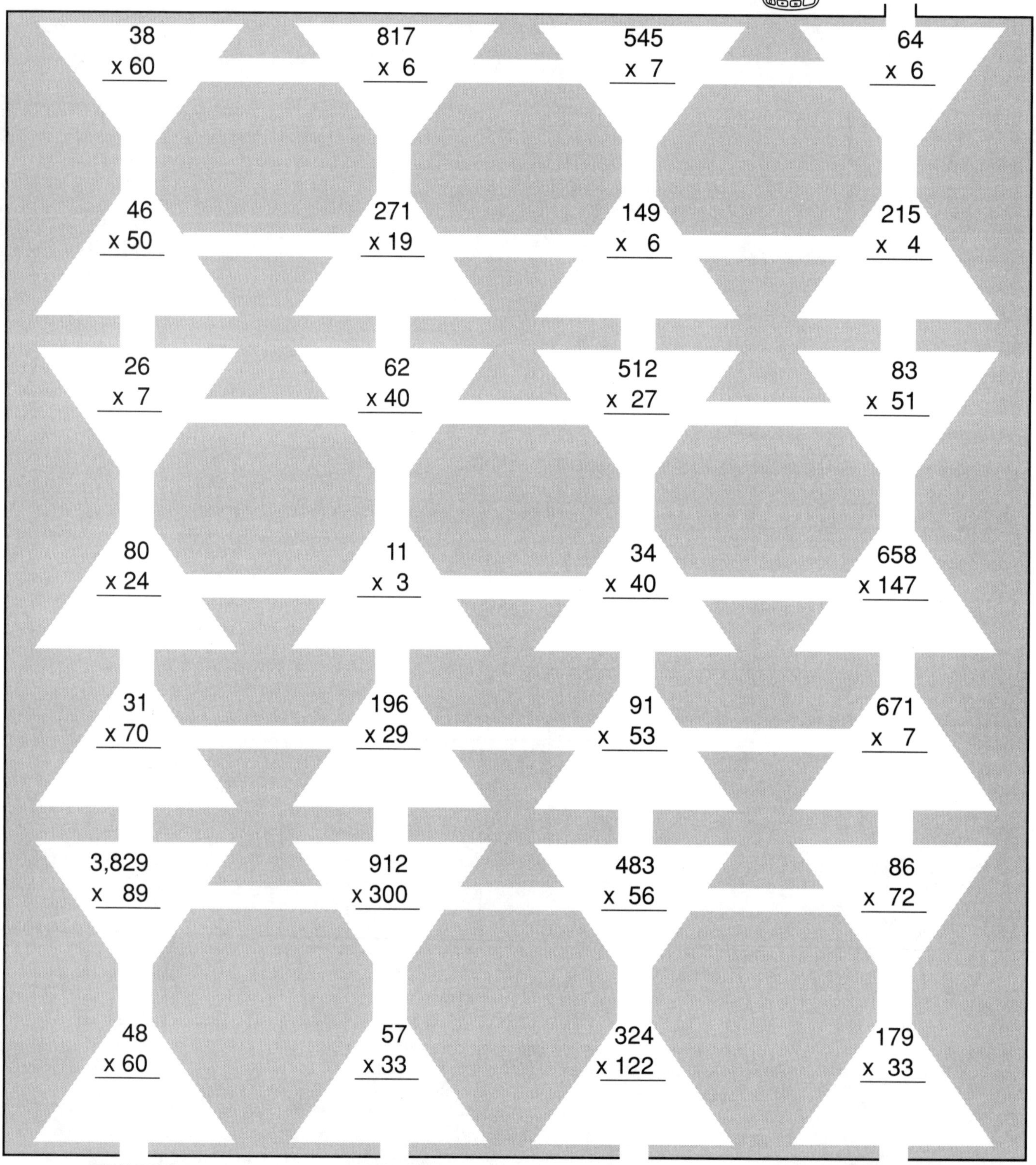

38 x 60	817 x 6	545 x 7	64 x 6
46 x 50	271 x 19	149 x 6	215 x 4
26 x 7	62 x 40	512 x 27	83 x 51
80 x 24	11 x 3	34 x 40	658 x 147
31 x 70	196 x 29	91 x 53	671 x 7
3,829 x 89	912 x 300	483 x 56	86 x 72
48 x 60	57 x 33	324 x 122	179 x 33

FINISH?   **FINISH?**   **FINISH?**   **FINISH?**

Bonus Box: Create your own multiplication maze on another sheet of paper. Give it to a friend to solve.

Name _____

The Groovin' Crew

Solve the problems. Show your work.

1. $6\overline{)703}$ 2. $9\overline{)229}$ 3. $8\overline{)8,954}$ 4. $5\overline{)608}$

5. $5\overline{)5,736}$ 6. $6\overline{)311}$ 7. $2\overline{)3,949}$ 8. $7\overline{)7,976}$

9. $8\overline{)677}$ 10. $6\overline{)833}$ 11. $5\overline{)6,432}$ 12. $9\overline{)389}$

13. $8\overline{)5,988}$ 14. $8\overline{)655}$ 15. $4\overline{)3,865}$ 16. $6\overline{)4,444}$

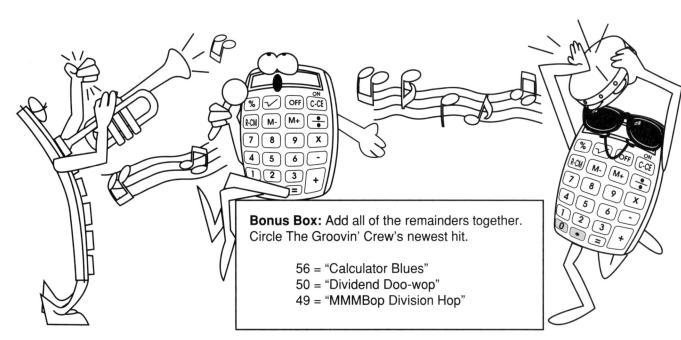

Bonus Box: Add all of the remainders together.
Circle The Groovin' Crew's newest hit.

56 = "Calculator Blues"
50 = "Dividend Doo-wop"
49 = "MMMBop Division Hop"

Name _____

Number Puzzles

Get ready to exercise your brain! Carefully read the directions for each number puzzle below. Then use your brainpower to solve each puzzle.

Complete the puzzle by arranging the even numerals 2–18 in the squares so that each row of three connected squares has the same total.

You Can Do It!

Complete the diamond by arranging the numerals 10–18 in the circles so that the sum of each line of circles is 42.

Good Luck!

Arrange the odd numerals 1–17 in the squares so that the sum of each line of squares is 36.

Give It A Try!

More Number Puzzles

Get ready to exercise your brain some more! Carefully read the directions for each number puzzle below. Then use your brainpower to solve each puzzle.

Solve this star of a puzzle by arranging the numerals 11, 12, 13, 14, 15, 23, 25, 26, 27, and 29 in the circles so that the sum of each straight line is 78.

Give It Your Best Shot!

Arrange the numerals 5–13 in the circles so that the sum of each row, column, and diagonal equals 27.

Use That Brainpower!

Use nine consecutive odd numerals of your choice to create your own puzzle. Arrange the numerals so that each row of circles has the same total.

Take The Challenge!

Name _____

Divide And Conquer

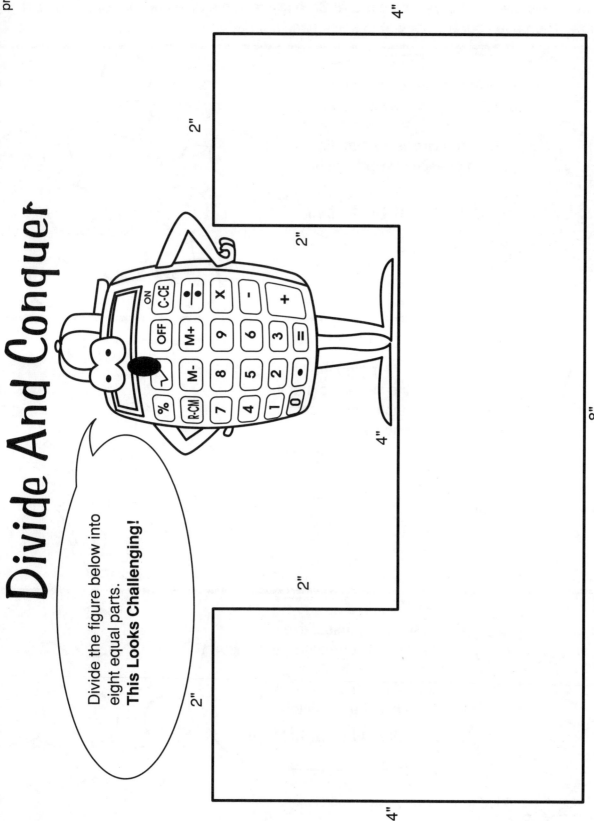

Divide the figure below into eight equal parts. **This Looks Challenging!**

2"

2"

4"

2"

2"

4"

4"

8"

Bonus Box: On the back of this sheet, create your own figure problem for a friend to solve.

National GARDEN MONTH

National Garden Month is celebrated throughout April to promote the cultivation of plants.

Plants make our homes and yards beautiful!

Plants provide oxygen that we need to live.

Gardening Greats

What's so great about gardens? Ask students why people enjoy gardening and what the benefits of cultivating plants are (see the examples shown). Supply a center with colorful flower cutouts, markers or crayons, and reference materials on plants and gardening. During free time, direct each student to the center. Have the student write a sentence answering the question "What's so great about gardens?" on one of the cutouts, then decorate it. Post each completed cutout on a bulletin board; then add green leaves, stems, and a white picket fence.

Noteworthy Nicknames

Foster a delight in the details of fanciful flowers by sharing the book *Fairy Dusters And Blazing Stars: Exploring Wildflowers With Children* by Suzanne Samson and Preston Neel (Roberts Rinehart Publishers, Inc.; 1994). While reading the story, have students point out the details from which each flower's name is derived. Next provide each student with a 9" x 12" sheet of drawing paper, markers or crayons, and reference materials. Assign each student a flower from the list below (or have the student choose one of his own). Then, using the book as a model, have the student rename the flower based on its unique features. Direct the student to draw a whimsical illustration and write a caption to accompany it. Afterward compile the pages and add a front and back cover. Bind the pages using lengths of yarn or brads; then share the book with other gung ho gardeners!

Baby bonnets protect babies from the summer sun. (Zinnias)

Flower Names

African violet	Hyacinth	Purple prairie clover
Arctic poppy	Hybrid tea rose	Pygmy bitterroot
Bunchberry	Ivy geranium	Round-lobed hepatica
California poppy	Larkspur	Soapweed
Cape jasmine gardenia	Lily of the valley	Tall bearded iris
Common sunflower	Morning-glory	Tawny-orange day lily
Daffodil	New York aster	Trailing arbutus
Dahlia	Pansy	Tuberous water lily
French marigold	Peony	Tulip
Garden nasturtium	Petunia	White evening primrose
Gloxinia		Zinnia

Planting The Seeds Of Learning

Cultivate a room full of master gardeners. Get some help in reaching this goal by contacting a local garden supply center. Invite a gardener from the center to speak to your class. Ask the gardener to demonstrate the various ways plants can be grown (from seeds, seedlings, and small cuttings). Have the gardener bring a supply of various seeds and discuss the growing conditions needed for each type of plant to grow properly. Afterward provide each student with the materials listed below and a copy of the directions. Have each student complete the activity as directed, and soon you'll see eager young gardeners sprouting up all over your classroom.

Materials For Each Student:
1 small milk carton with its top cut off, 1 pie pan, seeds, plastic wrap, 1 pencil, a sunny window, potting soil, water

Directions:
1. Poke two holes in the bottom of the milk carton with a pencil. Then fill the carton with potting soil.
2. Plant the seeds following the seed packet directions. Place the milk carton in the pie pan.
3. Gently water the soil until it is thoroughly moistened. Cover the container with plastic to help keep in the moisture. Place the container and its tray away from direct sunlight until the seeds have sprouted.
4. Water daily.
5. When the seedlings poke out, place the carton in a sunny window. Rotate the container daily to prevent the seedlings from bending toward the light.
6. Once the seedling has developed more than two pairs of leaves, it's ready for transplanting into a larger pot.

Ask The Expert!
Have your students become plant experts with the activity on page 16. Divide your students into pairs. Give each pair one copy of page 16; then assign the pair one of the questions below. Have each pair complete page 16 as directed.

1. What are the different types of gardens people grow?
2. What tools do I need to grow an outdoor garden?
3. What is the difference between a seed and a bulb?
4. Why do plants need soil to help them grow?
5. What are some of the things that I have to do to prepare outdoor soil for a garden?
6. How often should houseplants be watered?
7. What can I do to help fight diseases and pests that may harm my plants?
8. Why are weeds considered a problem, and what can I do to get rid of them?
9. What is mulch, and how does it help plants?
10. When do I know it's time to repot a houseplant, and how do I do this?
11. What is the difference between *annual, biennial,* and *perennial* plants?
12. What is pollination, and why does it occur?

How Does Your Garden Grow?

Green-thumbed Gill wants to plant a garden in his yard. He read a gardening book for information, but got a little confused when he wrote his notes. Each sentence he wrote is false. Read the information below; then rewrite each sentence to make it true. Gill also did not write his notes in order. Place the steps in the correct order by writing the appropriate numeral (1–10) in the box to the left of each step.

Planting An Outdoor Garden

There are several steps you need to take when planting an outdoor garden. First, choose a site for your garden. Make sure the area is well drained. Plants won't grow well in soggy soil. The site should also receive the proper amount of light. Many flowers and most vegetables need a large amount of light to grow. Second, prepare the soil. Use a shovel to remove the grass and other plants that cover the site. Dig up the soil about 8 to 12 inches; then break it up by turning it over and over. Add fertilizer if it is needed. Then run a rake over the soil to make it smooth. Next choose the plants you want to grow. It helps to sketch a garden plan before planting to avoid making mistakes. Make sure the plants grow well in your climate. When you are ready to plant, space the seeds apart so the plants will have enough room to grow. Planting vegetables in straight rows makes them easier to care for. Flowers look attractive if they are planted in irregularly shaped groups. After your garden is planted, water it when the soil is dry.

☐	Use a shovel to remove the grass, but keep all other plants.
☐	Water your garden so much that the soil never gets dry.
☐	Add fertilizer after you have raked the soil smooth.
☐	Most plants need a shady site to grow well.
☐	Dig up the soil no more than 8 inches.
☐	Plant vegetables in irregularly shaped groups so they can be cared for more easily.
☐	Choose a site where the water will keep the soil soggy.
☐	Space the seeds closely together so they don't grow all over the place.
☐	Choose plants that grow well in any climate.
☐	Draw a sketch of your garden after it grows to check for any mistakes.

Name(s) ______________________________

Ask The Expert!

Who better to ask than an expert when you need help growing a great garden! Imagine that you write a gardening column for a local newspaper. Research the answer to the gardening question your teacher gives you. Then respond to it in advice-column style. Write the question and your response in the space below; then draw an accompanying illustration in the box at the bottom right.

Gardener's Gazette

Gardening advice for the not-so-green-thumbed given by:
Garden ____________________
(Write your name here.)

Dear Garden ____________________,
(Write your name here.)

____?
(Write the question here.)

Signed, ____________________
(Write an imaginary name here.)

Dear ____________________,

(Write your response on the lines below.)

____

____

____

____

____

____

____

____

Sincerely,
Garden ____________________
(Write your name here.)

 Note To The Teacher: Use with "Ask The Expert!" on page 14.

NATIONAL HUMOR MONTH

April is National Humor Month. During this month focus on the joy of laughter and how it can enrich the quality of life.

Laugh It Up!

During National Humor Month, poll your students to find out what makes them laugh. Then have each of them write a story or draw a picture of a time when they laughed because they saw or heard something funny. Invite student volunteers to share their stories and/or pictures with the class.

Comic Combination

Kids love telling jokes and trading cards. Combine the two with the following activity: Duplicate one copy of page 18 for each student. Instruct each student to write one original joke or a joke that he's heard on each trading card. After students have completed their cards, have each student trade each card with a different person so that he ends up with three new joke cards from three different students. Allow enough time for each student to read these new joke cards; then have students trade again. After several trades, post the cards on a bulletin board for all to enjoy.

Silly Stories

Your students will be tickled pink with this fun writing activity. Write the following story starter at the top of each of four sheets of notebook paper: *Mrs. Frumplemeyer had just one thing to say when she found a rabbit munching on one of her prize tomatoes: "This means WAR!"* Divide your students into four groups. Give one person in each group one of the programmed sheets of notebook paper. Instruct that person to write one sentence to continue the story and then pass the paper on to the next student in the group. Have each group continue this process until each group member has written a sentence. Conclude the activity by reading each group's story. Your students will be amazed at how different and funny each story turns out.

What runs all day, but never runs away?

A clock.

SHARE-A-JOKE TRADING CARD

_____
(name of student)

_____

_____

_____

_____

_____

_____

Is this an original joke?   Yes ☐ No ☐

If "No," where did you hear the joke? _____

©1998 The Education Center, Inc. • _April Monthly Reproducibles_ • Grades 4–5 • TEC950

SHARE-A-JOKE TRADING CARD

_____
(name of student)

_____

_____

_____

_____

_____

_____

Is this an original joke?   Yes ☐ No ☐

If "No," where did you hear the joke? _____

©1998 The Education Center, Inc. • _April Monthly Reproducibles_ • Grades 4–5 • TEC950

SHARE-A-JOKE TRADING CARD

_____
(name of student)

_____

_____

_____

_____

_____

_____

Is this an original joke?   Yes ☐ No ☐

If "No," where did you hear the joke? _____

©1998 The Education Center, Inc. • _April Monthly Reproducibles_ • Grades 4–5 • TEC950

Name _____

Write Your Own Comic Strip

A comic strip is a humorous short story that is told in a series of illustrated scenes. Comic strips appear in weekly and daily newspapers. Think about what you enjoy the most about your favorite comic strip. Then create your own comic strip in the spaces below. If a character speaks, be sure to put his or her words in speech bubbles similar to these: ☁☁   Color each scene.

1.	2.	3.
4.	5.	6.

Bonus Box: Write the name of your favorite comic strip on the back of this page. Then write a brief paragraph explaining why you like this comic strip.

Note To The Teacher: Share with your students your favorite comic strip(s), as well as a variety of other appropriate comic strips, before having them begin the above activity.

An Original Knock-Knock Joke

By

_____

(student)

1. "Knock-knock."

2. "Who's there?"

3. "_____."

4. "_____?"

5. "_____."

"Knock-Knock!" "Who's There?"

Everybody loves a good laugh. Complete the rib-tickling activity below to exercise your mind as well as your funny bone.

Directions: Read the two sample "knock-knock jokes" below. Then create your own original joke in the form at the right. After you've written your joke, cut along the dotted line to separate your joke from these directions.

WHO'S THERE?

Examples:

1. "Knock-knock."

   "Who's there?"

   "Les."

   "Les who?"

   "Les go! What's taking you so long?"

2. "Knock-knock."

   "Who's there?"

   "Harry."

   "Harry who?"

   "Harry up! We'll be late for the movie."

20

Note To The Teacher: Distribute one copy of this page and a pair of scissors to each student. Have each student complete the page as directed. Post all the jokes on a bulletin board for students to read and enjoy.

National Poetry Month

National Poetry Month was founded in April 1996 by the Academy of American Poets. Its purpose is to celebrate poetry and its importance in our lives. For a current update on the festivities held in April, as well as for resources about poetry and poets, check out the Academy's Web site at *www.poets.org/npm/npmmain.htm.*

Popping With Poets

Put your students to work on a project that will have your room popping with poets! Supply a center with the following materials: a selection of poetry anthologies, biographical references, light-colored construction paper, 4" x 6" index cards, a eight-inch paper-doll cutout for each pair of students, glue, and markers or crayons. Pair students. In turn, direct each pair to the center. Have each pair select a different poet and poem. Instruct the pair to copy the poem onto a sheet of construction paper and draw a decorative border around it. Then have the pair research the poet and write a brief informational paragraph about him or her on an index card. Finally have the pair decorate a paper-doll cutout and attach the index card to the cutout as shown. After the pair shares its project, use clothespins to attach the cutout and poem to a string that has been stretched across the classroom.

Poetic Announcements

Add a little style to your school's morning announcements with the following poetry-promoting project! Arrange with the school principal to have your students read their favorite poems aloud over the school intercom. Each morning throughout the month, send a different reader to the office to share her poem. If desired, use an instant camera to take a snapshot of the reader before or after her reading. Then glue each picture to a colorful star cutout and post it in a hallway display. While your students are basking in their five minutes of fame, they'll be improving their oral-reading skills and sharing an enjoyment of poetry with others.

The Land Of Happy

Shel Silverstein

Shel Silverstein was born in 1932 in Chicago, Illinois. He started writing and drawing when he was young. His first job was drawing cartoons. He says he hopes people of all ages find something to like in his books.

Stately Poets

Inspire your budding poets with a stately occasion they'll not soon forget! Since 1668, Britain's king or queen has appointed a *poet laureate,* or official poet. This person serves for life and is expected to write formal poems for special occasions. Many U.S. states have their own poet laureates. Contact your state government to inquire if your state has one. Then have your class write a special poem about your state. Send the poem to your state's poet laureate, along with an invitation for him or her to visit your school. If your class receives a positive response, have your students plan a special poetry reading for the honored guest.

Mixin' Up A Concrete Poem

Who ever said writing a **concrete** poem was hard stuff? This type of poem simply shows words written in the shape of a picture. For example, the words in a poem about love might be written in the shape of a heart. Look at the example below. What do you think the poem is about?

Example:

sweet
colorful circles
that   are
lots   of
fun to share
yummy

Directions:

1. Choose a noun (person, place, thing, or idea).
2. Brainstorm a list of words that describe the noun. Write the words in the space below.
3. On a sheet of construction paper, write the words in the shape of a picture that depicts the noun.
4. Use markers or colored pencils and other arts-and-crafts materials to add decorative details to your poem.

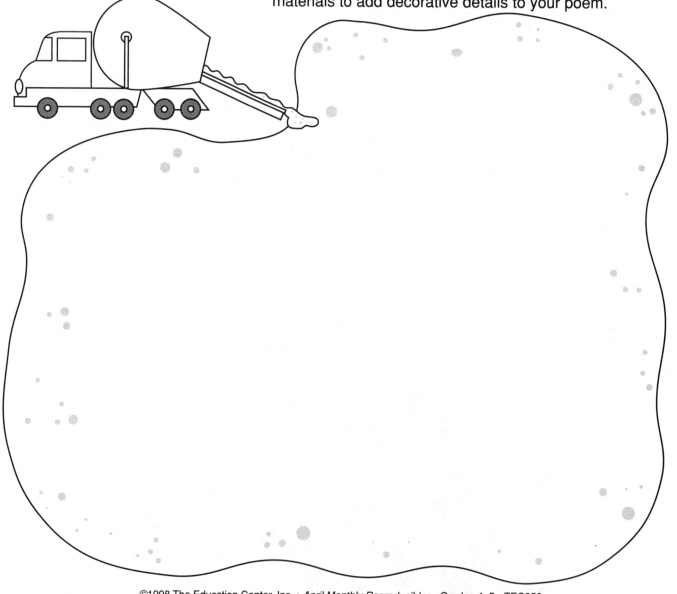

Note To The Teacher: Provide each student with a 9" x 12" sheet of light-colored construction paper, markers or colored pencils, glue, and various arts-and-crafts materials. **Note:** *The answer to the question in the above introduction is LifeSavers® candy.*

Name _____

Getting The Message Across!

An **acrostic** poem uses each letter of its subject to begin each line of the poem. Acrostic poems are about people, places, things, or ideas. Each line tells something about the poem's subject. Read the example shown.

Directions:

1. Choose a subject for your poem.
2. Cut out the pattern below. Use this pattern to trace a rectangle on a piece of tagboard for each letter in your subject. Cut out the tagboard rectangles.
3. Write each letter in your subject on a different cutout.
4. Write each line of your poem on one of the cutouts. Be sure to begin each line with the letter shown. Add decorative details to your cutouts with crayons or markers.
5. Use the hole puncher to make a hole at the top and bottom of each cutout (see Figure 1).
6. Create a mobile by connecting each cutout with lengths of yarn. (See Figure 2.). Hang your mobile in a special spot.

Example:

Feasts of color on

Long green stems

Outdoors, indoors

Wonderful scents

Ever lovely and

Refreshing

Special plants

Figure 1

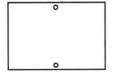

Figure 2

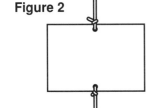

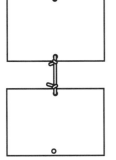

Note To The Teacher: Provide each student with tagboard, scissors, crayons or markers, a hole puncher, and six-inch lengths of yarn.

Tickle Your Funny Bone!

A **nonsense** poem may not make much sense, but it does have rhythm and rhyme. Read the examples below.

Examples:

Blueberries are red;
Strawberries are blue;
Salt is sweet;
How about you?

Woses are wed;
Wiolets are wlue;
Wugar is weet;
And woe are wue!

Directions: Have some fun with nonsense poetry by taking a verse of another poem and changing some of the words or letters. Write a different version of the poem on each bone below. Then cut out these shapes along the bold lines and share some nonsense with your classmates!

Name _____

An Eye For Haiku

A **haikū** is a type of poem from Japan. These poems are usually about simple things in the world around us, especially nature. The poem has three short lines. The first and third lines are about the same length and a little shorter than the second line. The poem does not have to rhyme.

Directions:

1. Think of an object in nature.
2. Imagine that your eye is like the lens of a camera and you are taking a picture of this object with your eye.
3. On the lines below, write what you *see, smell, hear, feel,* and *taste.*
4. Use your observations to help you write your own haiku on the camera lens below.
5. Draw a picture on the camera to accompany your poem. Then color and cut out your camera.

Example:

sunlight
splashing rainbows
in a puddle

I see: _____

I smell: _____

I hear: _____

I feel: _____

I taste: _____

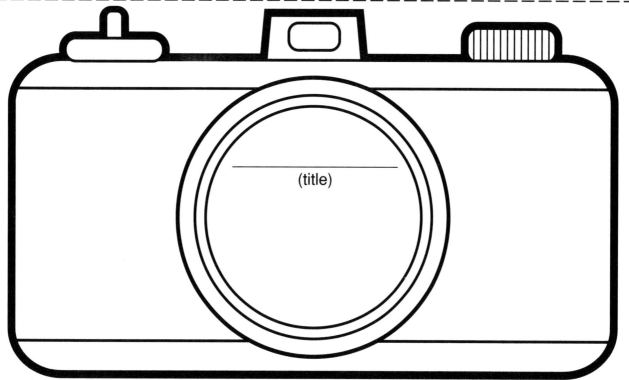

(title)

Note To The Teacher: Provide each student with markers or colored pencils and scissors. Post completed poems on a display titled "An Eye For Haiku."

Bloomin' Good Poetry!

A *cinquain* is a poem with five lines. The lines follow a pattern like the example below.

Line 1 subject (one word)
Line 2 two words to describe the subject
Line 3 three action verbs each ending in *ing*
Line 4 four words to describe feelings about the subject
Line 5 synonym for subject (one word)

Example:

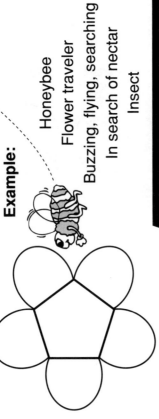

Honeybee
Flower traveler
Buzzing, flying, searching
In search of nectar
Insect

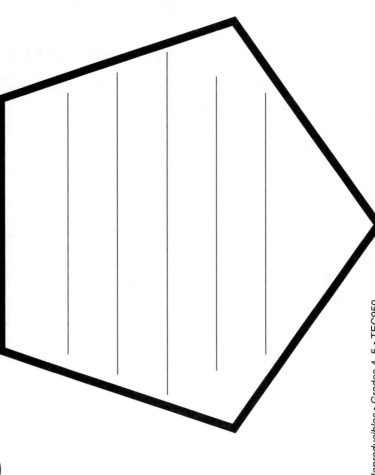

Directions:

1. Choose a spring-related subject. Write at least three facts about this subject.

2. Decide how you want to order your facts; then write each line of your poem on the lines in the pentagon shape at the right.

3. Cut out the pentagon shape and glue it to the center of a 9" x 12" sheet of construction paper.

4. Draw five petals around the pentagon shape. Decorate these petals using markers or colored pencils and arts-and-crafts supplies.

5. Cut out your flower. Tape a plastic straw on the back of it and "plant" it in your class's poetry garden.

©1998 The Education Center, Inc. • *April Monthly Reproducibles* • Grades 4–5 • TEC950

Note To The Teacher: Provide each student with markers or colored pencils, scissors, glue, a 9" x 12" sheet of colorful construction paper, various arts-and-crafts supplies, tape, and a plastic straw. Prepare a display, such as a bulletin board or a gardening pot filled with a Styrofoam® block, in which students can plant their flowers.

National SCHOOL LIBRARY Month

In addition to National School Library Month, many other library and reading events and celebrations are held during the month of April. National Library Week is observed the week of the first Sunday in April, International Children's Book Day is held each year on April 2, Hans Christian Andersen's birthday is April 2, and Reading Is Fun Week is observed the third week of April.

Cyberspace Field Trip

Take a field trip into cyberspace by having your students explore the following book- and reading-related Web sites.
(Web sites were current as of May 1998.)

http://scholastic.com
http://scholastic.com/goosebumps/index.htm
http://scholastic.com/magicschoolbus/index.htm
http://scholastic.com/babysittersclub/index.htm
http://www.thecase.com/kids
http://www.readin.org/thereadin/default.html

Library List Poems

In honor of National School Library Month, have each student create a library list poem. Assign each student one of the library-related terms from the box below. Instruct each student to write his word vertically on a sheet of notebook paper. Then have the student write a word or phrase that begins with each letter in his assigned library term. Tell students that the words or phrases should create one long sentence when read aloud. Write the following example on the board as a model for students.

> Latasha went
> Into the library to check out a
> Book to
> Read
> And she saw her buddy
> Rusty reading Old
> Yeller.

Community Project

There are many organizations in your community that would love a donation of children's books. Have students bring in books that they no longer read and do not wish to keep. Also ask the school librarian for any books that she would like to discard. Select which community organization(s) should receive the books. Have students repair loose pages or torn covers. Then give each student one bookplate pattern (see page 28) for each donated book. Have each student fill out and decorate each pattern with markers or crayons. Then instruct the student to paste one bookplate inside each donated book. Arrange a special class field trip to deliver the books.

Word Box

book	quiet	overdue	volumes
hardcover	card catalog	fines	storyteller
paperback	magazines	reference	mystery
shelves	novels	research	adventure
spine	nonfiction	atlas	science fiction
pages	fiction	dictionary	fantasy
checkout	biographies	encyclopedia	library card
librarian			assistant

Patterns

Use with "Community Project" on page 27.

This book has been donated to

_____
(name of organization)

by

_____
(student)

_____   _____
(age)   (grade)

_____
(name of school)

_____
(date)

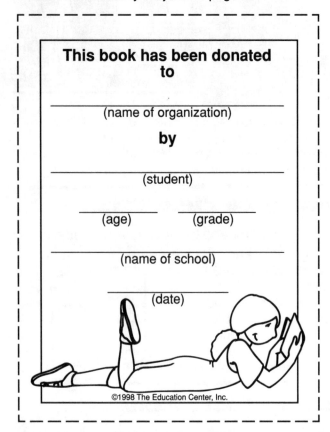

©1998 The Education Center, Inc.

This book has been donated to

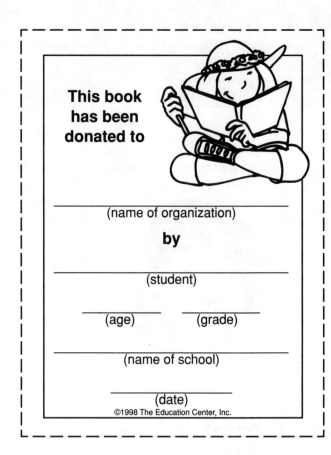

_____
(name of organization)

by

_____
(student)

_____   _____
(age)   (grade)

_____
(name of school)

_____
(date)

©1998 The Education Center, Inc.

This book has been donated to

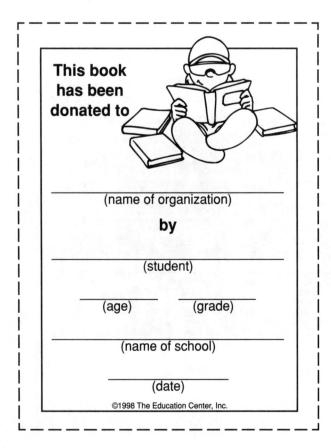

_____
(name of organization)

by

_____
(student)

_____   _____
(age)   (grade)

_____
(name of school)

_____
(date)

©1998 The Education Center, Inc.

This book has been donated to

_____
(name of organization)

by

_____
(student)

_____   _____
(age)   (grade)

_____
(name of school)

_____
(date)

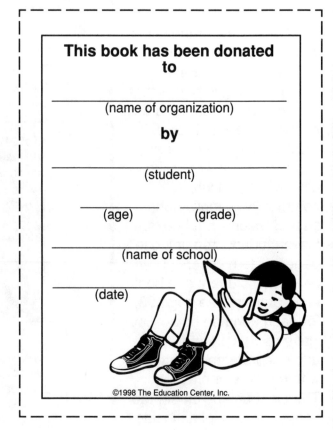

©1998 The Education Center, Inc.

©1998 The Education Center, Inc. • *April Monthly Reproducibles* • Grades 4–5 • TEC950

28   **Note To The Teacher:** Instruct students to cut out their bookplates by cutting carefully along the dotted lines.

Can't Judge A Book By Its Cover

It's true that you can't judge a book by its cover, but a well-planned cover sure can make a reader want to pick up a book. Complete the following activity to create a cover for your favorite book.

1. Think of your favorite book—one that you may have read several times—and write its title here:
   _____

2. Write a brief paragraph in the box below that summarizes what you found so exciting or captivating about this book.

3. Using a four-star rating scale, rate your favorite book in each category below.
   ★ = Poor, ★★ = Satisfactory, ★★★ = Great, ★★★★ = Fantastic

   _____ Plot
   _____ Interesting characters
   _____ Excitement
   _____ Kept my attention
   _____ Suspenseful ending
   _____ Humorous

4. Create a book cover for your favorite book. Be sure to include the title of the book, the author's name, and an illustration that will make readers want to pick up the book and begin reading.

Dewey Decimal Scavenger Hunt

In 1876 Melvil Dewey developed a system of classifying books in libraries. This system is still used today. No matter which library you visit, you can easily find a book if you know how to use the Dewey Decimal System.

With a partner, locate each Dewey Decimal classification category listed in the boxes below. Write the name of one book found in that section in the box directly beneath the appropriate category. Can you locate all ten categories?

Generalities 000–099	Natural Sciences And Mathematics 500–599
Philosophy And Psychology 100–199	**Technology And Applied Sciences** 600–699
Religion 200–299	**The Arts** 700–799
Social Sciences 300–399	**Literature** 800–899
Language 400–499	**Geography And History** 900–999

Bonus Box: How long has the Dewey Decimal System been in existence if it was first published in 1876?

©1998 The Education Center, Inc. • *April Monthly Reproducibles* • Grades 4–5 • TEC950

Note To The Teacher: Work with your school librarian to complete this activity. Divide your students into pairs. Give each pair one copy of this page. To make the scavenger hunt more exciting, place a brightly colored strip of paper in a book in each section. Give each pair that finds a hidden strip a special prize.

National School Library Month: graphic organizer

Book-Talk Map

GENRE: _____

TITLE: _____

AUTHOR: _____

SETTING

TIME: _____

PLACE: _____

CHARACTERS

CRITIQUE

RESOLUTION OF CONFLICT (CONCLUSION)

CONFLICT (PLOT)

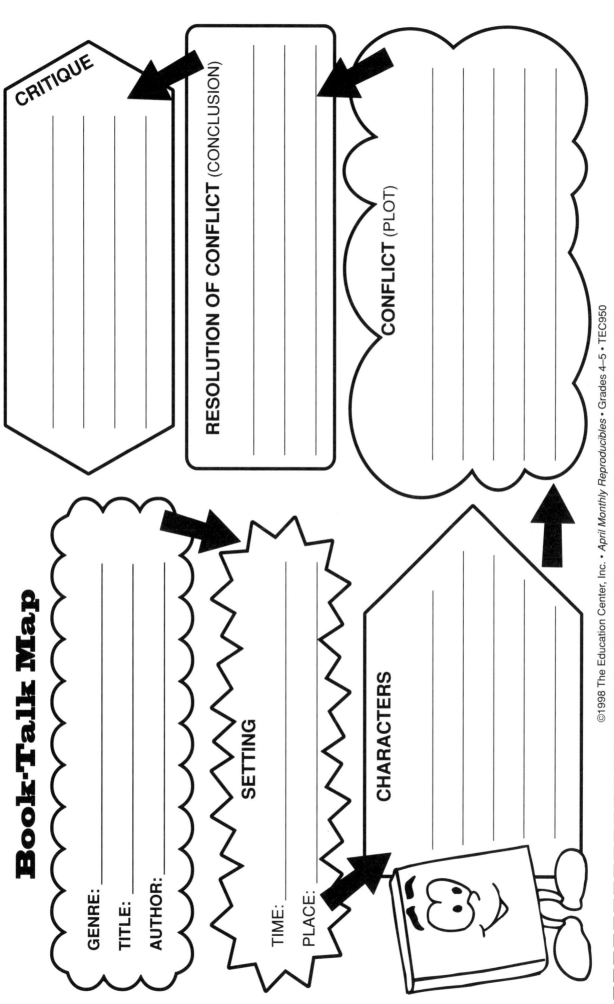

Note To The Teacher: Divide your students into six groups. Assign each group a different reading genre such as realistic fiction, science fiction, fantasy, adventure, mystery, or historical fiction. Instruct each student in each group to find one novel in the school library that fits the assigned genre. Have each student prepare an oral presentation on his book to present to the rest of the class. Have him fill in the Book-Talk Map above to use as notes during his presentation.

Major-League Cities

On April 14, 1910, President William Howard Taft started a sports tradition by throwing out the first baseball of the season, helping to make the game a national pastime. So, swing into baseball season and National School Library Month with this cool research activity.

Directions: Select a U.S. city that is home to a major-league baseball team. Then go to the library to research the information in the glove below.

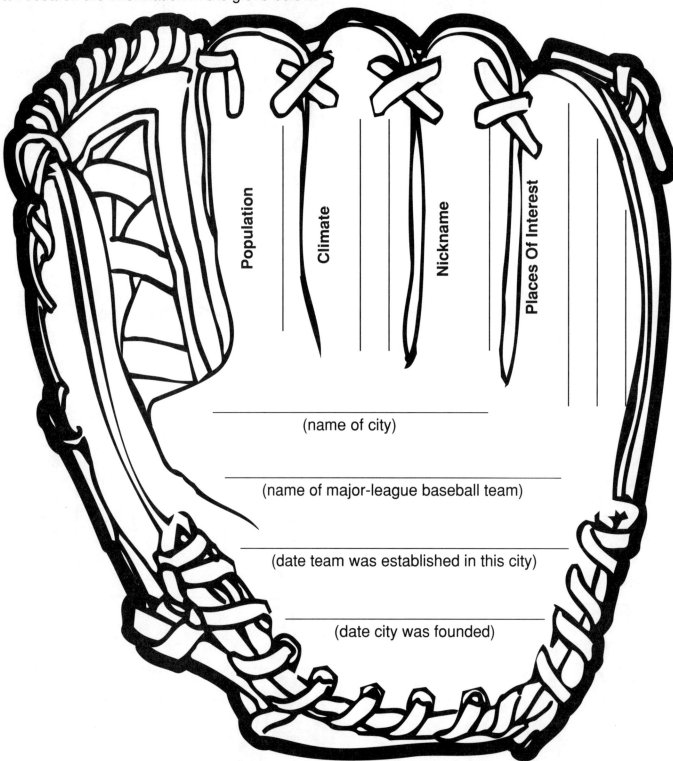

Population

Climate

Nickname

Places Of Interest

_____
(name of city)

_____
(name of major-league baseball team)

_____
(date team was established in this city)

_____
(date city was founded)

Bonus Box: On the back of this page, list any records held by the baseball team listed in the glove above.

National
READING A ROAD MAP DAY

National Reading A Road Map Day is celebrated annually on April 4. The purpose of this special day is to encourage present and future drivers to view map reading as an enjoyable pastime and a survival skill.

BEEP BEEP!

Nifty Facts About Roads And Maps

Take a little time to learn about the history of roads and maps with the following activity. Begin by drawing a large timeline on the board that spans from A.D. 150 to 1960. Write each fact about roads and maps on a separate index card. Then shuffle the cards and distribute one to each pair of students. Ask each pair to read its card to the class, then place it on the timeline.

- About 150, Ptolemy, the Egyptian scholar, used mathematics to make maps of the world for the first time.
- In 1507, a German cartographer named Martin Waldseemüller made the first map using the term "America" for the new lands.
- Captain John Smith published a map of Virginia's coastline in 1612.
- One important early American road, the Wilderness Road, was marked out by Daniel Boone in 1775.
- The Lancaster Turnpike, the first hard-surfaced road, was completed in Pennsylvania in 1794.
- In 1891, the International Geographical Congress proposed the mapping of the entire world on a scale of 1:1,000,000—a job that still has not been accomplished!
- The first State Highway Department was established in 1891 by the New Jersey state government. State highway departments are responsible for controlling local road construction and development.
- The first freeway, which was completed in Germany in 1921, was only six miles long.
- The federal interstate highway system was begun in 1956. The system is designed to allow drivers to travel from coast to coast and border to border without an intersection or a traffic light.
- In 1960, the United States had 951,100 miles of dirt roads and 2.17 million miles of surfaced roads.

Maps, Maps, Marvelous Maps!

Maps come in different shapes and sizes, and are used for different purposes. However, maps also have many similarities. Help students identify the similarities and differences between maps with this easy-to-do activity. Collect a variety of maps from local auto clubs. Divide students into small groups and provide each group with two different maps. Pose the following questions for groups to ponder as they study the maps:

- What do the maps have in common?
- How are the maps different?
- What can you learn about a place by reading and studying a map of the area?
- What do you find interesting about the maps?

Conclude the activity by having each small group present its findings to the class.

Pack Your Bags And Let's Go!

Challenge students to apply their map-reading skills with this adventurous activity! Direct each student to choose a place that he would like to visit within your region. Next have the student use regional road maps to chart the course to his destination. Have the student be specific in detailing the directions, the names of roads traveled, and the names of major cities or sites passed along the way. Extend the activity by having each student determine the total number of miles traveled.

(Check with your State Department of Transportation, your State Highway Patrol, or an auto club for regional road maps.)

How Far Is It?

A map *scale* shows you how far it is between two points on a map. For example, the scale may show that one inch on the map equals ten miles on Earth. If two places are three inches apart on the map, they are really 30 miles apart on Earth (10 miles x 3 inches).

A. Complete the table below to determine the real-life distances using the given scales.

Scale	2 inches = ? miles	2 1/2 inches = ? miles	5 inches = ? miles	10 inches = ? miles
1 inch = 8 miles				
1 inch = 10 miles				
1 inch = 50 miles				
1 inch = 100 miles				

B. Study the map below; then use the scale and a ruler to measure the distance asked for in each question. Remember that the roads are not completely straight so you must follow the curve of the road! Write your answers on the lines provided.

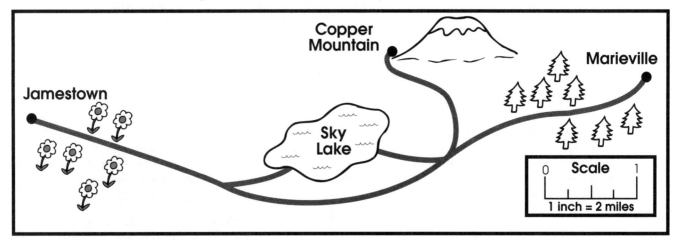

1. What distance does one inch equal on this map? _____

2. How far is the drive from Jamestown to Copper Mountain? _____

3. How many miles will you have to travel to reach Sky Lake from Marieville? _____

4. If you drive from Marieville to Jamestown, how many miles will you travel? _____

5. Is Marieville or Jamestown closer to Sky Lake? _____

6. By how many miles is it closer? _____

Bonus Box: If you were traveling at 40 miles per hour, how long would it take you to travel from Jamestown to each place on the map?

Cartographer's Challenge

A *cartographer* is a mapmaker. Use your mapmaking skills to complete the map below. Carefully study the symbols in the *legend* before beginning. Then draw each symbol on the map according to the directions below.

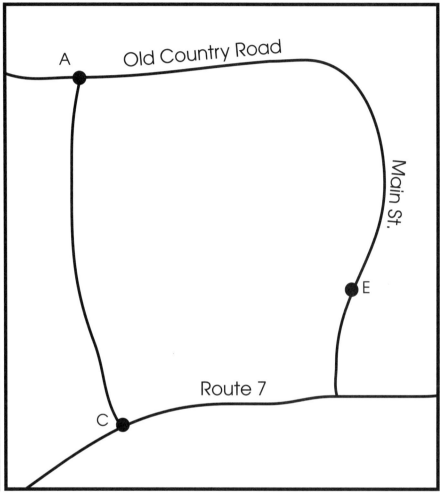

1. There is a lake located between Town A and Town E.
2. Town B is located on the road south of Town A, 10 miles north of Town C.
3. There is a mountain in the northeast corner of the map.
4. A hiking trail goes from the mountain to the lake.
5. A picnic area is on the east side of the lake, southeast of the trail.
6. A forest is north of the lake and south of Old Country Road.
7. Lake Road runs between Town B and Town E.
8. The airport is located in an open area west of Town B.
9. Town D is located at the intersection of Main Street and Route 7.
10. The hospital is five miles west of Town D, on the south side of the road.
11. The police and fire stations are about five miles south of Town E, one on each side of Main Street.
12. A school is located about two miles southeast of Town A.
13. Go back over the directions and check your map.

Bonus Box: On the back of this sheet, write a paragraph describing the area shown on the map. Be sure to include in your paragraph place names, what it's like to live there, and what people do for fun and work.

Road Map Scavenger Hunt

So you think you're an expert on reading road maps? Find out just how good a mapreader you really are by completing this scavenger hunt with a partner.

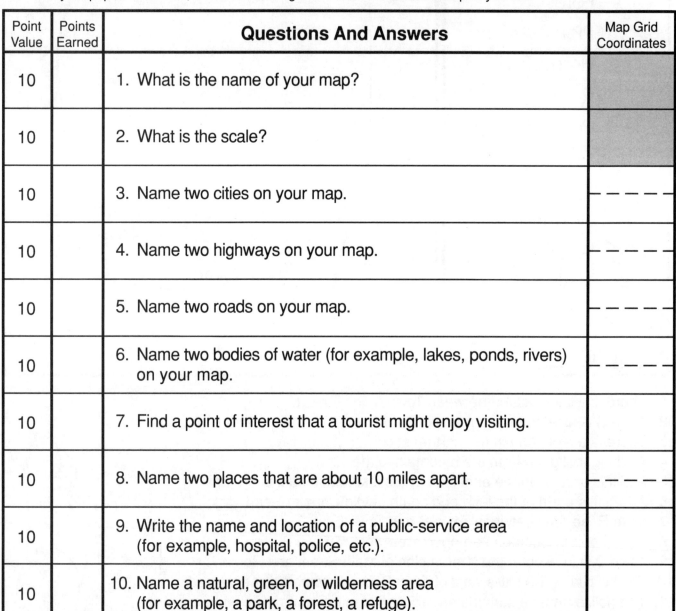

Scoring Chart
100 = Wonderful Road Warrior
90 = Terrific Traveler
80 = Knowledgeable Navigator

Directions:

1. Use the road map your teacher gives you to answer each item below.
2. Write the grid location coordinates for items 3–10 in the spaces provided.
3. When you and your partner are finished, trade maps and papers with another team. Check the team's responses and award 10 points for each correct answer.
4. After your paper is returned, check the Scoring Chart to see what kind of expert you are.

Point Value	Points Earned	Questions And Answers	Map Grid Coordinates
10		1. What is the name of your map?	
10		2. What is the scale?	
10		3. Name two cities on your map.	_ _ _ _ _
10		4. Name two highways on your map.	_ _ _ _ _
10		5. Name two roads on your map.	_ _ _ _ _
10		6. Name two bodies of water (for example, lakes, ponds, rivers) on your map.	_ _ _ _ _
10		7. Find a point of interest that a tourist might enjoy visiting.	
10		8. Name two places that are about 10 miles apart.	_ _ _ _ _
10		9. Write the name and location of a public-service area (for example, hospital, police, etc.).	
10		10. Name a natural, green, or wilderness area (for example, a park, a forest, a refuge).	

TOTAL:

Bonus Box: Draw a map of your neighborhood, including important or interesting sites. Also make a legend or key for your map.

©1998 The Education Center, Inc. • *April Monthly Reproducibles* • Grades 4–5 • TEC950

NATIONAL WEEK OF THE OCEAN

National Week Of The Ocean is celebrated in April. This week is set aside to remind us that the ocean is something we should appreciate, protect, and use wisely.

Taking Care Of The Ocean

An oil spill in the ocean can be a major disaster for marine life. Help students better understand the effects of an oil spill with the following activity:

Materials For Each Of Five Groups Of Students: 1 feather per student (obtainable from craft shops), 1 paper towel per student, 1 small plastic cup partially filled with water, 1 small plastic cup partially filled with motor oil, 2 eyedroppers

Steps:
1. Divide students into five groups and distribute the materials. Have each student place his feather atop the paper towel.
2. In turn, have each group member place a drop of water on his feather and carefully observe the results. Next have him place a drop of oil on a dry area of his feather and carefully observe the results.
3. Ask students how the water and the oil each affected the feathers. Point out that oil coats things it comes in contact with, which makes it difficult to remove.
4. Discuss how an oil spill can be harmful to seabirds and other marine life. Explain that even though most countries ban the dumping of waste oil by ships at sea, dumping still occurs, as do accidental oil spills.

Colorful Creatures

From blowfish to lobsters and sharks to starfish, the ocean has it all! Have students make beautiful sea creatures of their own with this art project. Enlarge the ocean-creature patterns on page 38. Then duplicate a class supply of the patterns. Have each student select a pattern to cut out. Then have the student trace this cutout onto black construction paper and carefully cut on the resulting outlines without cutting through the area outside these outlines. Have the student discard the center, cut-out piece and set aside the remaining stencil. Next have the student paint a solution of diluted white glue onto a sheet of white construction paper the same size as the black sheet of paper. Then glue different-colored tissue-paper squares onto the white construction paper. When the white paper is completely covered with squares, direct the student to glue the black construction-paper stencil on top of it, aligning the edges. While the glue is drying, challenge each student to research to find three to five facts about his chosen ocean creature. Finally have the student use either a white colored pencil or a white crayon to write these facts around his colorful sea animal.

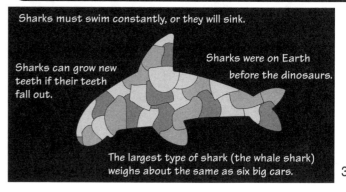

Sharks must swim constantly, or they will sink.

Sharks can grow new teeth if their teeth fall out.

Sharks were on Earth before the dinosaurs.

The largest type of shark (the whale shark) weighs about the same as six big cars.

Patterns

Use with "Colorful Creatures" on page 37.

Journey To The Bottom Of The Sea

Imagine that you are in a submarine traveling to the ocean floor. As you descend, you pass through different ocean layers. The deeper you go, the darker and colder it becomes.

Directions: Research a different animal found in each zone. Draw a picture of that animal in that section of the submarine window at the left. Then, in the notebook on the right, write facts about each animal, such as its size, coloring, special physical features, eating habits, and defenses.

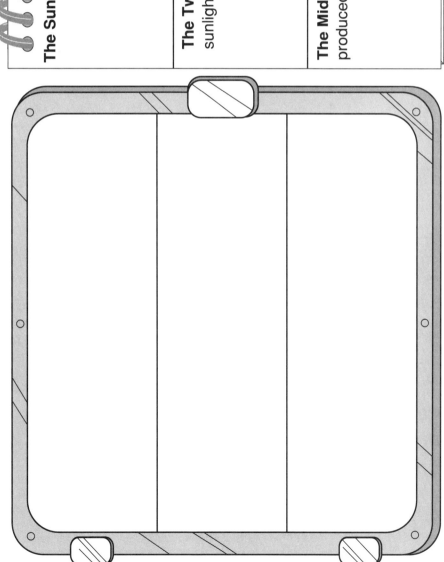

The Sunlight Zone: 0 to 600 feet; receives the most sunlight

The Twilight Zone: 600 to 3,000 feet; receives very little sunlight

The Midnight Zone: 3,000 to about 15,000 feet; its only light produced by bioluminescence

Note To The Teacher: Provide students with reference materials and crayons or colored pencils.

Name_____ National Week Of The Ocean: reading a bar graph, math vocabulary

 **Seagoing Sizes**

The oceans are full of animals of all shapes and sizes—from the smallest crab to the largest whale. Study the bar graph and then read the problems below. Fill in each blank with a word or phrase from the Word Bank that completes the problem. Use each word or phrase only once.

Animal Lengths In Feet

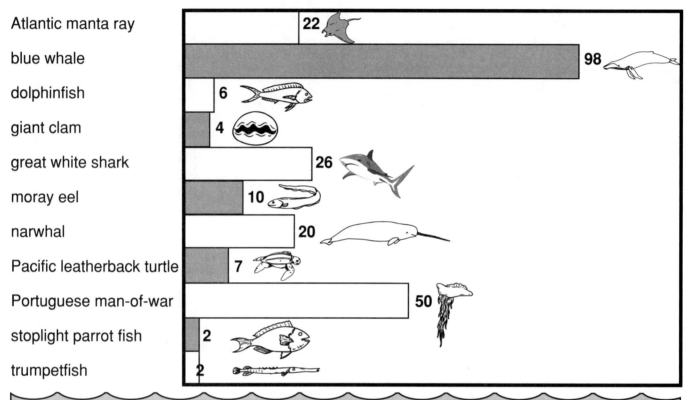

Word Bank

greater than	total	twice	three times	less than
half	more than	in all	equal	same

1. A blue whale is almost _____ as long as a Portuguese man-of-war.

2. A moray eel is _____ the size of a narwhal.

3. The length of a dolphinfish is almost _____ to the length of a Pacific leatherback turtle.

4. The great white shark is _____ 20 feet long.

5. The stoplight parrot fish and the trumpetfish are the _____ length.

6. The _____ length of a giant clam and blue whale is 102 feet.

7. A dolphinfish is _____ the size of a trumpetfish.

8. The length of the Atlantic manta ray is _____ that of a narwhal.

9. The length of the Pacific leatherback turtle is _____ six of the other animals.

10. The total length of a giant clam, great white shark, and narwhal is 50 feet _____.

Bonus Box: Choose an animal from the bar graph above. On the back of this sheet, list as many objects as possible that are about the same length as this animal.

40   ©1998 The Education Center, Inc. • *April Monthly Reproducibles* • Grades 4–5 • TEC950 • Key p. 64

ASTRONOMY WEEK

Astronomy Day is observed sometime between mid-April and mid-May on a Saturday near or before the first quarter moon. Astronomy Week begins on the Monday before Astronomy Day.

A Planetary Excursion

All aboard for a planetary excursion that is out of this world! Divide your class into eight teams. Assign each team a different planet, not including Earth. Provide each group with a variety of space-related reference materials. Instruct each group to research the unique characteristics and special features of its assigned planet. Next have each group use this information to create travel posters or brochures promoting its planet. Have the group include unusual sights that a tourist might see while visiting the planet. Direct each group to include creative as well as factual information in the travel guide. Have each group present its travel poster or brochure to the class. Allow students to vote on their favorite planetary vacation spots!

Mission To Mars

The United States and the Soviet Union have had many cooperative space projects, including Apollo-Soyuz. Once a cosmonaut and an astronaut met in Mars, Pennsylvania, to talk to school groups about their experiences in space and other U.S.-Soviet space efforts. Have your students use atlases to find towns named for planets and other celestial bodies, such as Venus and Jupiter, Florida; Earth and Mercury, Texas; and Neptune, New Jersey.

Discovering Jupiter

No one has ever seen the surface of Jupiter—the largest planet in the solar system—because the gases in its atmosphere shield the planet from full view. These gases also form the bands around the planet known as *belts.* Jupiter's surface gravity is 2.87 times greater than Earth's. That means a person weighing 100 pounds on Earth would weigh 287 pounds on Jupiter. Challenge your students to calculate how much they would weigh on Jupiter. Provide a basic bathroom scale so each student can measure his own weight. Instruct each student to multiply his weight by 2.87. Then have each student use the chart below to calculate how much he would weigh on each of the other planets. Students won't be able to "weight" to work these math problems!

Mercury	.38
Venus	.90
Mars	.38
Saturn	1.07
Uranus	.93
Neptune	1.23
Pluto	.03?

Name _____

In Search Of A Star

A star is a humongous ball of glowing gas. Our sun is a star. Astronomers believe that there are billions and billions of stars in the universe! However, the universe is not the only thing full of stars. Many of the words we use every day contain the letters *s-t-a-r*. Complete the activity below to see how many starry words you can find.

Directions: The answer to each clue below contains the letters *s-t-a-r*. Read each clue; then fill in the missing letters for each mystery word.

Clues	Mystery Words
1. a vehicle on rails that is used to transport people on city streets	s t _ _ _ _ _ _ a r
2. a person who is extremely talented with great public appeal	_ _ _ _ _ _ s t a r
3. an official recorder or keeper of records	_ _ _ _ _ s t _ a r
4. a tall and powerful working dog of a Swiss alpine breed	S t. _ _ _ _ _ a r _
5. an instance of suffering from extreme hunger	s t a r _ _ _ _ _ _ _
6. clean and free of germs	s _ _ _ t a r _
7. an official marking on a piece of mail	_ _ s t _ a r _
8. the room where worship services are held	s _ _ _ _ t _ a r _
9. an invertebrate with five arms that lives in the ocean	s t a r _ _ _ _ _
10. a long, narrow, wavy strip that floats in the wind	s t _ _ a _ _ r
11. a loved one	s _ _ _ t _ _ a r _
12. a series of steps for passing from one level to the next	s t a _ r _
13. a person whose job is to manage routine and detail work for a superior	s _ _ _ _ _ t a r _
14. adequate; being enough	s _ t _ _ _ a _ _ _ r _
15. to frighten or surprise	s t a r _ _ _ _
16. a red, juicy fruit	s t _ a _ _ _ r _ _

Bonus Box: Use the dictionary to find five more words that contain the letters *s-t-a-r*. List those words on the back of this sheet.

Agreeing With Astronomy

You have to agree—astronomy is fascinating! Each sentence below is not only a fascinating fact about astronomy, but each contains a subject and verb, too. If the subject in a sentence is *singular,* you must use a *singular* verb. If the subject in a sentence is *plural,* you must use a *plural* verb. That way the subject and verb will agree with one another.

Directions: Read each sentence below. Circle the subject and underline its verb in each sentence. Next decide if the correct form of the underlined verb has been used. If you *agree,* color the first star at the end of the sentence. If you *disagree,* color the second star at the end of the sentence. The first one is done for you.

	Agree	Disagree
1. (Stars) shine by their own light.	T	Q
2. Cliffs and craters scars the surface of Mercury.	C	E
3. The Sun moves across the sky as Earth rotates.	Y	F
4. Earth tilts as it orbits the Sun.	R	L
5. We lives on the only planet that seems to support life.	K	S
6. A scientist measure distances in the universe in light years.	D	N
7. The Moon's gravity cause Earth's tides to rise and fall.	Y	A
8. Rusty-red rock covers the surface of Mars.	Z	G
9. A huge storm cloud rages constantly on Jupiter.	M	H
10. Icy particles makes up the narrow ringlets that circle Saturn.	V	J
11. Uranus orbits the Sun once every 84 years.	W	X
12. Poisonous clouds swirl around Neptune.	I	B
13. Pluto spends 248 years orbiting the Sun once.	O	U

Solve this mystery sentence by writing the letter that you colored for each number shown below.

___ ___ ___ ___ ___ ___ ___ ___ ___   ___ ___   ___ ___ ___ ___ ___ ___ ___ !
7 5 1 4 13 6 13 9 3   12 5   7 11 2 5 13 9 2

Bonus Box: On the back of this sheet, write two sentences about astronomy. Be sure that your subjects and verbs agree.

Name _____

A Cosmic Contract

Have a little fun with these far-out activities on astronomy!
Color each star or planet when you complete its activity.

_____ activities = Awesome Astronomer
_____ activities = Outstanding Observer
_____ activities = Satisfactory Stargazer

I WENT TO EARTH AND ALL I GOT WAS THIS SILLY SHIRT

1. You have been selected to live in a space station for a year. You are only allowed to bring five items with you. List the items you are taking and explain why you chose each one.

2. Read several myths about constellations. Then create a constellation of your own and write a myth to explain it.

3. Create a poem that describes one of the nine planets.

4. Construct a model of a space shuttle and other craft objects. On an index card, list its major craft components and a brief description of each.

5. Using unlined index cards, design a set of postcards, one for each planet. Label and illustrate a different planet on the front of each postcard; then write five facts about the planet on the back of the postcard.

6. Listen to the movie soundtrack of a space-related movie, such as *Star Wars* or *Star Trek*. As you listen to the music, paint or sketch one or more images that come to mind.

7. Make a collage featuring astronomy-related pictures and illustrations.

8. Make a timeline that shows at least ten important dates in space travel.

9. Write a journal entry that might have been written by an astronaut during a trip to the moon.

10. Research the birth and death of a star. Create a poster that shows the life cycle of a medium-sized star such as our sun.

11. Make a chart that describes the composition, the atmosphere, and the size of each planet.

12. Research the following famous astronomers: Copernicus, Galileo, and Ptolemy. Write a brief paragraph about each one describing his contribution to the science of astronomy.

44

©1998 The Education Center, Inc. • *April Monthly Reproducibles* • Grades 4–5 • TEC950

Note To The Teacher: Program a copy of the contract and choose a reward, such as a special treat or privilege, for each level of completion. Then duplicate a copy of the contract for each student. Have the student select the number of activities he will complete. After the student meets his goal, treat him with the designated reward.

Thomas Jefferson's Birthday

Thomas Jefferson was born on April 13, 1743. Jefferson is best known for writing the Declaration of Independence and serving as the third president of the United States. But he also loved farming, botany, music, law, mathematics, and architecture, just to name a few of his many interests.

The Louisiana Purchase

Big Dreams

Thomas Jefferson had big dreams for the United States. He wanted to double the size of the country by buying millions of acres of land from France. Jefferson accomplished his dream and it's known as the Louisiana Purchase. Divide your students into small groups. Duplicate one copy of page 46 and 47 for each group. Have each group complete the map on page 46 by following the directions on page 47 to learn more about this historical event.

Macaroni Pie

Thomas Jefferson became fond of macaroni while visiting in Italy. He brought this version of the recipe to the colonies. In Jefferson's version of the recipe, he uses white or yellow cheese. Yellow cheese was very uncommon in Italy but was very common in the colonies. So most likely the macaroni and cheese dish we enjoy eating today is a descendent of Jefferson's recipe. Recruit parent volunteers to help you prepare Jefferson's Macaroni Pie for the classroom. Follow the recipe below and enjoy!

Paleontology Pursuit

Did you know that Thomas Jefferson loved *paleontology?* Turn your students into junior *paleontologists* with the following activity. Divide your students into pairs. Duplicate one copy of page 48 for each pair. Also supply each pair with one sheet of poster board, scissors, and crayons or markers. Instruct each pair to use available reference materials as well as materials in the library to complete the activity.

Ingredients:
2 cups uncooked macaroni
salt
1/4 pound grated white or yellow cheese
1/4 pound butter or margarine, melted

Directions:
Place the uncooked macaroni into a large pot of boiling, salted water. Boil the macaroni until barely tender. Drain. Mix the pasta with the cheese and butter or margarine, and place in a baking dish. Bake at 350° for about 15 minutes or until the cheese is melted and bubbly. Makes 5–6 servings.

The Louisiana Purchase

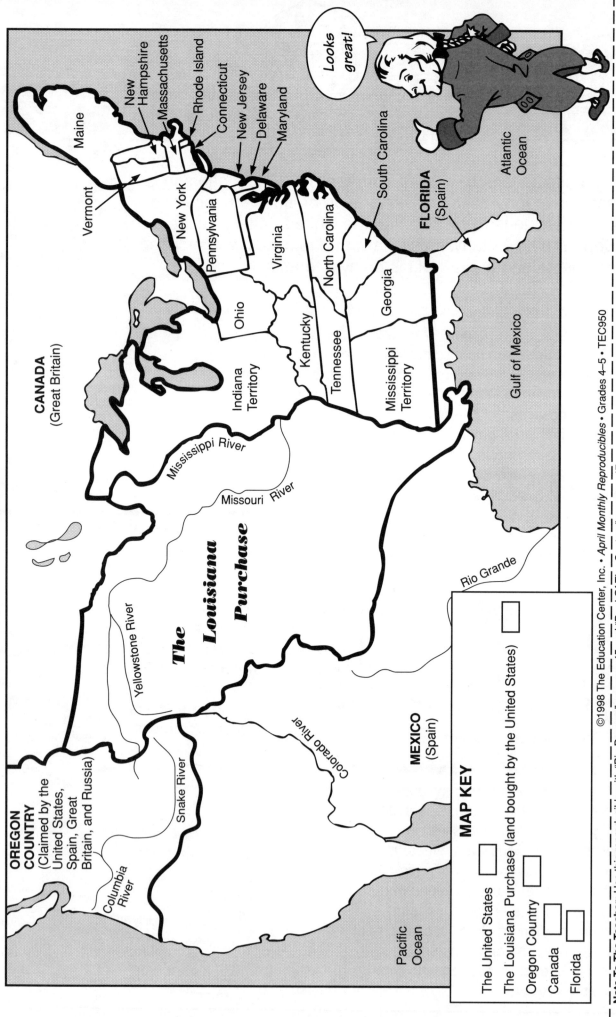

Note To The Teacher: Use this reproducible with "Big Dreams" on page 45 and "Deal Of The Century" on page 47.

Deal Of The Century

Some might say that Thomas Jefferson made the "deal of the century" (the nineteenth century) when he purchased millions of acres of land from France. The price paid was $15 million. This averaged out to be about four cents an acre! This deal is known as the Louisiana Purchase. Research to complete the activities below.

Activity 1

At the time of The Louisiana Purchase, the United States consisted of the original 13 colonies, Vermont, Maine, Ohio, Kentucky, Tennessee, the Indiana Territory, and the Mississippi Territory. Color this area of your group's map yellow. Be sure to also color-code the map key. Then mark the location of Washington, DC, with this symbol: ✪.

Activity 2

In 1804, Florida was still owned by Spain. Color Florida green on your group's map and color-code the key. Florida was founded and named by the Spanish explorer, Ponce de León. Ponce de León heard tales of a fountain of youth, but he never found it. On the back of this sheet, write a brief description of what life would be like if you discovered the fountain of youth.

Activity 3

The Oregon Country was located in what is today the northwestern corner of the United States. Color the Oregon Country blue on your group's map and color-code the key. On the blanks below, list the states that were formed from the land originally known as the Oregon Country.

1. _____

2. _____

3. _____

Activity 4

Our neighbor to the north, Canada, was owned by Great Britain during the time of the Louisiana Purchase. Color Canada orange on your group's map and color-code the key. The Canadian city of Quebec was founded by a country other than Great Britain. Citizens of Quebec today still speak the language of its original founders. Research to find the name of the country that explored Canada and settled Quebec before the British.

Activity 5

Jefferson doubled the size of the United States with the Louisiana Purchase. Color the area of the Louisiana Purchase purple on your group's map and color-code the key. Research to find the names of at least three states today that were formed from the land of the Louisiana Purchase.

1. _____

2. _____

3. _____

Activity 6

In 1804, Thomas Jefferson sent Meriwether Lewis and William Clark on an expedition to explore Louisiana. They left St. Louis, Missouri, with a crew of 47 soldiers, woodsmen, and trappers. At the great bend of the Missouri River, Lewis and Clark hired a French-Canadian fur trapper and his wife, Sacajawea—a Shoshone Indian—to be their guides. Research to find the route taken by Lewis and Clark. Trace their route on your group's map with a red marker.

Note To The Teacher: Use this reproducible with "Big Dreams" on page 45 and "The Louisiana Purchase" on page 46.

Paleontology Pursuit

Thomas Jefferson loved *paleontology,* the study of fossils and the remains of prehistoric life. If Jefferson were alive today, you just might find him at a dinosaur dig investigating these awesome creatures of the past.

Directions: Research to find out in which time period—the *Triassic Period,* the *Jurassic Period,* or the *Cretaceous Period*—each dinosaur listed at the bottom of the page lived. Then complete the prehistoric road below by writing each dinosaur's name in the appropriate time period.

Directions: Select one dinosaur from the prehistoric road at the left and re-search to complete the information below.

1. Name of dinosaur: _____

2. Time period in which it lived: _____

3. Location (the country in which fossils/remains have been found): _____

4. Weight: _____

5. Height or Length: _____

6. Is this dinosaur a plant eater, a meat eater, or both? _____

7. Write a brief description of the dinosaur. _____

8. Draw an illustration of the dinosaur in the box below.

The Triassic Period, 245–208 million years ago

1. _____
2. _____
3. _____

The Jurassic Period, 208–144 million years ago

4. _____
5. _____
6. _____
7. _____

The Cretaceous Period, 144–66 million years ago

8. _____
9. _____
10. _____

Triceratops   Iguanodon
Stegosaurus   Staurikosaurus
Pteranodon   Seismosaurus (unofficial name)
Tyrannosaurus   Plateosaurus
Allosaurus   Chasmatosaurus

Note To The Teacher: Use this reproducible with "Paleontology Pursuit" on page 45.

NATIONAL COIN WEEK

National Coin Week is celebrated the third week in April.
This is a time to promote the hobby of coin collecting.

Coining New Coins

Challenge your students to name who appears on each of the U.S. coins. *(Lincoln—penny, Jefferson—nickel, F. D. Roosevelt—dime, Washington—quarter, Kennedy—half dollar, Eisenhower—silver dollar).* Then explain that sometimes special coins are minted to honor famous people or to celebrate historic events. Have each student imagine that he has been chosen to design a new quarter, dime, nickel, and penny. Explain that each design must represent something special that has happened in his life. Give each student an enlarged copy of the coin patterns on page 50 on which to create his final designs. Next have the student cut out each coin and use a hole puncher to make holes in each coin. Direct the student to use six-inch lengths of yarn to connect the coins as shown. Allow each student to share his coins; then suspend them from the ceiling for an attractive display.

Coin Toss

Have students practice making change with this partner game. Divide your class into groups of 3 or 4 students. For each group tape a small bowl to the floor. Then affix a strip of tape to the floor approximately five steps away from the bowl. Place a variety of coins in a container next to the strip of tape. To play, one student sits by the bowl and is designated to be the *counter*. The remaining students are the *coin tossers.* In turn, each coin tosser randomly picks two coins, stands on the tape strip, announces the value of each coin, and tries to toss each coin into the bowl. If a coin goes in, the counter adds the value of the coin to his count. If a coin misses the bowl, the coin is not counted. After each coin tosser has tossed his coins, have the counter subtract his coin total in the bowl from five dollars. If he is correct, he earns a point. Change counters and a new round of play begins.

Patterns

Use with "Coining New Coins" on page 49.

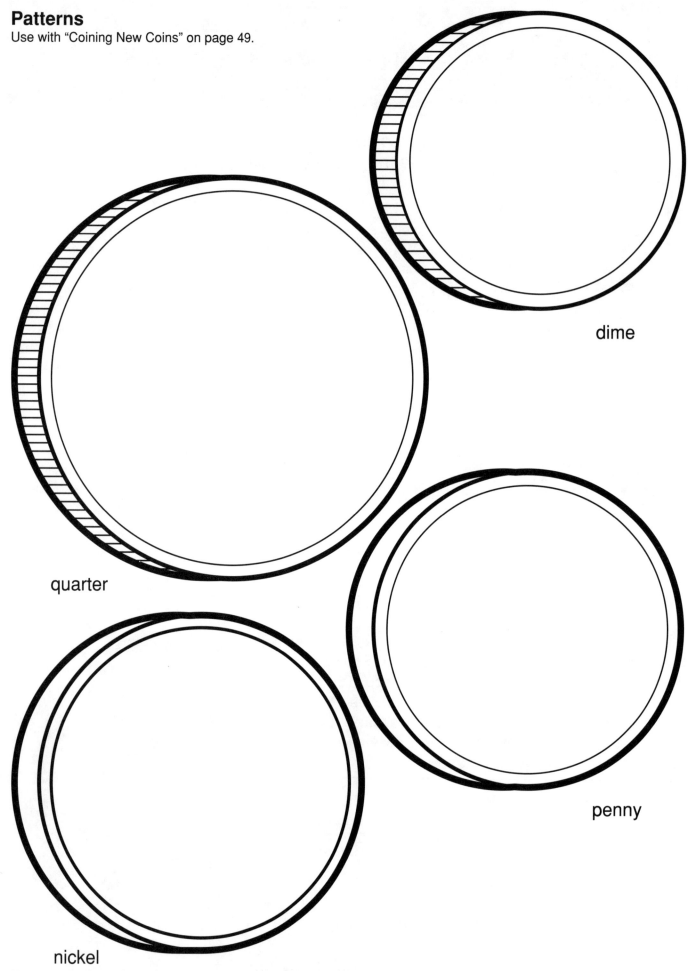

dime

quarter

penny

nickel

Coin Capers

Follow the directions to complete each coin challenge below.

1.

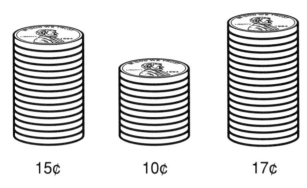

15¢   10¢   17¢

Describe how you would make each stack have the same number of pennies.

2. There are 14 different combinations to make $0.65 using quarters, dimes, and nickels. On the back of this paper, make an organized list naming each combination.

---

3. Cut out the coin patterns below. Place a dime, penny, nickel, and quarter on the spaces shown. Pretend that the coins are stacked on top of each other in a tower. You want to move all four coins, one at a time, to Column C so that they are in the same order as in Column A. What are the fewest number of moves you need to make? Two rules to remember:

• You can't move a coin if there's another coin on top of it in a tower. For example, you can't move the penny from Column A until you have moved the dime that is on top of it.

• No coin can be placed above one that is smaller in size. For example, the penny cannot be stacked above the dime.

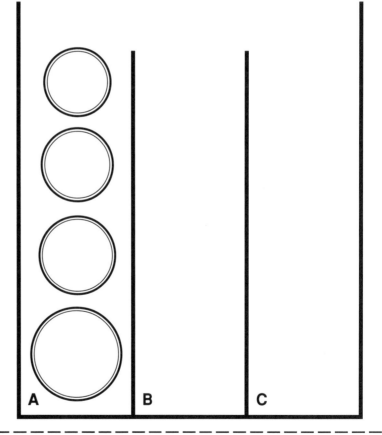

Note To The Teacher: Provide each student with scissors.

Coins Of The World

Sure you're familiar with the U.S. coins, but how about coins from around the world? The names of other countries' coins are hidden in the grid below. To discover the names of these coins, write the letter for each ordered pair of numbers in the blanks below. The first one has been started for you.

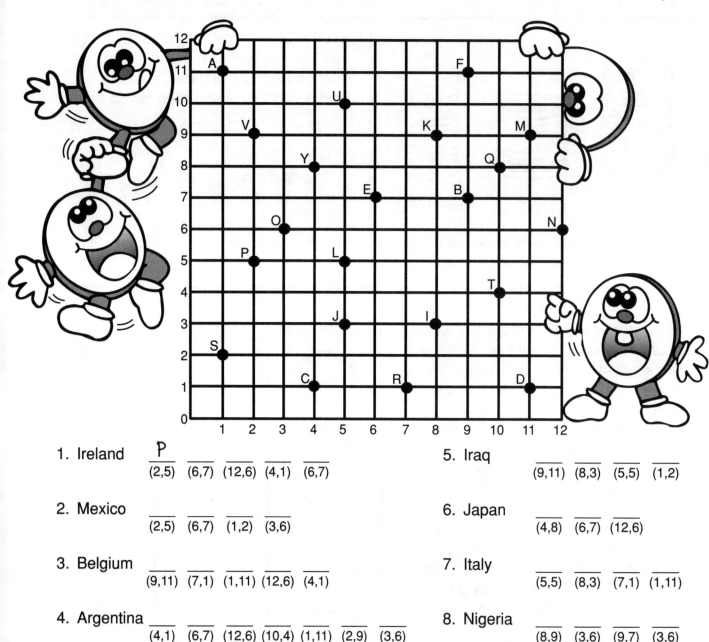

1. Ireland $\underset{(2,5)}{P}$ $\underset{(6,7)}{\quad}$ $\underset{(12,6)}{\quad}$ $\underset{(4,1)}{\quad}$ $\underset{(6,7)}{\quad}$

2. Mexico $\underset{(2,5)}{\quad}$ $\underset{(6,7)}{\quad}$ $\underset{(1,2)}{\quad}$ $\underset{(3,6)}{\quad}$

3. Belgium $\underset{(9,11)}{\quad}$ $\underset{(7,1)}{\quad}$ $\underset{(1,11)}{\quad}$ $\underset{(12,6)}{\quad}$ $\underset{(4,1)}{\quad}$

4. Argentina $\underset{(4,1)}{\quad}$ $\underset{(6,7)}{\quad}$ $\underset{(12,6)}{\quad}$ $\underset{(10,4)}{\quad}$ $\underset{(1,11)}{\quad}$ $\underset{(2,9)}{\quad}$ $\underset{(3,6)}{\quad}$

5. Iraq $\underset{(9,11)}{\quad}$ $\underset{(8,3)}{\quad}$ $\underset{(5,5)}{\quad}$ $\underset{(1,2)}{\quad}$

6. Japan $\underset{(4,8)}{\quad}$ $\underset{(6,7)}{\quad}$ $\underset{(12,6)}{\quad}$

7. Italy $\underset{(5,5)}{\quad}$ $\underset{(8,3)}{\quad}$ $\underset{(7,1)}{\quad}$ $\underset{(1,11)}{\quad}$

8. Nigeria $\underset{(8,9)}{\quad}$ $\underset{(3,6)}{\quad}$ $\underset{(9,7)}{\quad}$ $\underset{(3,6)}{\quad}$

Use the grid to write the ordered pairs of numbers for the U.S. coins named below.

1. quarter ____ ____ ____ ____ ____ ____ ____

2. dime ____ ____ ____ ____

3. nickel ____ ____ ____ ____ ____ ____

4. penny ____ ____ ____ ____ ____

The first Earth Day was celebrated on April 22, 1970, with the motto "Give Earth A Chance." Observances focused on the need to reclaim the purity of our air, water, and living environment.

Keep America Beautiful Month

Earth Day occurs during Keep America Beautiful Month. In honor of both events, have your students brainstorm tasks they can do to help protect the nation's environment. Then have them each pick one task to do after school. The next day ask each student to share details of his good deed. Afterward give each student a piece of poster board on which to create an illustrated sign detailing his task performed "to Keep America Beautiful." For example: "I picked up trash in the schoolyard to Keep America Beautiful" or "I recycled glass bottles to Keep America Beautiful." Have each student write this challenge at the bottom of his sign: "What will *you* do to help today?" Post the signs around the school to promote awareness of Keep America Beautiful Month and Earth Day.

Trash Weigh-In

On average, each American produces about three pounds of trash each day! Help students determine how much trash they produce each week. Instruct each student to collect his family's trash in one or more trash bags for one week and weigh each bag of trash collected to get a total weight. At the beginning of the following week, have each student report the weight of his family's trash collected from the previous week. Record the weights on the board. Then have your students determine the average weight of one family's trash for a week based on the class's data.

Did I make all this trash?

Wild And Rare

Around the world hundreds of plants and animals are threatened with becoming extinct. Help your students learn more about some of these plants and animals by having them work in pairs to complete the following activity. Give each pair one copy of page 57. Duplicate page 56 and cut out each illustrated animal; then assign each pair of students one of the animals to research and give them the corresponding animal illustration. Instruct each pair to use a variety of reference materials to complete the needed information at the top of page 57. Have each pair use the bottom half of page 57 to write a brief plan of action to help save its assigned endangered animal. Post each pair's work on a bulletin board titled "Wild And Rare."

What A Waste!

Have you ever thought of how much paper and plastic are used to package the meals you purchase at your favorite fast-food restaurants? To determine which of your favorite fast-food restaurants produces the most waste, complete the chart below each time you buy a fast-food meal during the month of April. Try to keep your purchases similar at each restaurant. For example, if you buy one burger, one order of fries, and one drink at McDonalds®, then when you go to Burger King® you should also buy one burger, one order of fries, and one drink.

Name Of Fast-Food Restaurant	number of paper bags	number of paper cups	number of Styrofoam® cups	number of napkins	number of plastic utensils (forks, spoons, knives)	number of Styrofoam® sandwich/burger containers	number of paper/foil sandwich/burger wrappers or containers	number of french-fry bags/cartons	number of plastic straws	number of condiment packets (ketchup, mayonnaise, salt, etc.)	total pieces of trash
(Restaurant #1)											
(Restaurant #2)											
(Restaurant #3)											
(Restaurant #4)											
(Restaurant #5)											

Bonus Box: Look at the data in your chart. Then, on the back of this sheet, write a paragraph telling which restaurant is most environmentally friendly and why.

©1998 The Education Center, Inc. • *April Monthly Reproducibles* • Grades 4–5 • TEC950

Note To The Teacher: Give each student one copy of this page at the beginning of April. Instruct each student to complete the chart each time he or she visits a different fast-food restaurant during the month of April. At the end of the month, have students bring in their charts to compare data.

Burning Rain

Sometimes rain contains chemicals that can harm animals and even damage buildings, but can it harm plant life too? Complete the project below to determine the effects of acid rain on plants.

Materials:

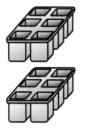

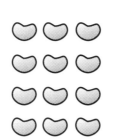

- 2 bedding-plant trays with 6 compartments each
- 1 cookie sheet
- 12 large lima beans
- water
- vinegar
- potting soil

Directions:

Step 1: Place the two bedding-plant trays on a large cookie sheet. Fill each compartment of both bedding-plant trays with soil.

Step 2: Soak the lima beans overnight; then plant them in the trays. Water normally until germination occurs (the first leaves sprout).

Step 3: Sprinkle one set of plants daily with ordinary water; sprinkle the other set with a mixture of one part water and one part vinegar. (Make sure the liquid wets the leaves and the soil.)

Step 4: At the end of each week, write your observations of the two sets of plants in the chart below. Be sure to note any differences in size, number of leaves, color, or appearance. After four weeks write your conclusions about the effects of acid rain on plants.

Week	Plants Sprinkled With Water	Plants Sprinkled With Vinegar/Water

Conclusions: _____

_____

_____

_____

_____

Dugong

Bald Eagle

Numbat

Green Pitcher Plant

Black-Footed Ferret

Small Whorled Pogonia Orchid

Brown Hyena

Loggerhead Sea Turtle

Indian Python

Grevy's Zebra

Aye-Aye

Jaguar

(Glue animal illustration here.)

Wild And Rare

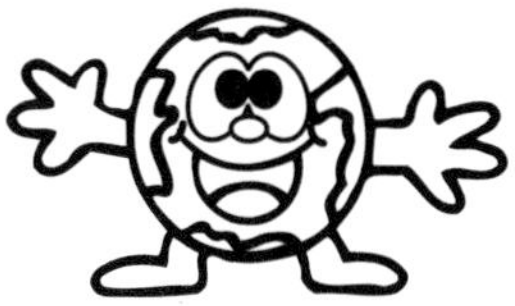

Animal Name: ______________________

Location: ______________________

Feeding Habits: ______________________

Cause(s) Of Endangerment: ______________________

Measures Taken To Prevent Extinction: ______________________

Plan Of Action

How We Can Help Save This Endangered Animal From Extinction

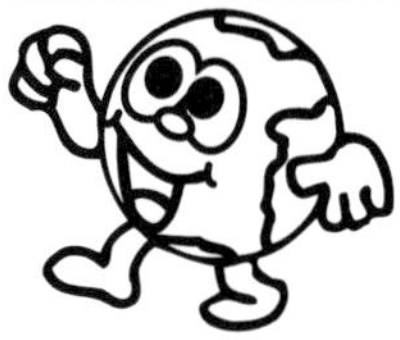

Note To The Teacher: Use with "Wild And Rare" on page 53.

Earth-Smart Inventions

Items that we use every day—such as automobiles, televisions, VCRs, and computers—use gasoline or electricity. In the box at the right, create a new invention or modify an existing invention so that it does not pollute the environment in order to operate. Maybe your invention could use wind power, solar power, or human power.

ARBOR DAY

Arbor Day celebrates the importance of trees to our environment by encouraging people to plant them. The first Arbor Day was celebrated in Nebraska on April 10, 1872, through the efforts of a newspaper publisher named Julius Sterling Morton. Arbor Day was later changed to April 22 in honor of Morton's birthday. Most states and many countries celebrate this day, although not on the same date.

A Forest Full Of Friends

Who hasn't enjoyed the friendship of a lovely tree? Have students share the different types of trees found in their yards, such as oaks, dogwoods, or palms. Ask students to point out their favorite details about their trees. Then provide each student with a 12" x 18" sheet of drawing paper and markers or colored pencils. Instruct each student to imagine that she can have any type of tree she'd like in her yard or near her home. Then direct the student to research that type of tree and illustrate it, showing the tree's special characteristics. Encourage the student to add details to the illustration about how she'd enjoy her tree, such as sitting under it reading a book, playing on a tire swing, or observing the various animals and insects that make the tree their home. Post the illustrations on your classroom walls to create a beautiful forest.

Operation Fruit Bowl

Turn a lesson on seeds into an Arbor Day celebration. Prior to your lesson, gather a variety of fruit, such as apples, grapes, peaches, and oranges; a paring knife; clear plastic cups; and potting soil. Cut open one of each type of fruit and remove the seeds. Show students the different seeds, having them share their observations about each type. Next use the information at the bottom of this page to discuss how seeds sprout into trees. Then divide students into groups based on the number of different fruits donated. Have each group fill a plastic cup with potting soil, then plant a different seed in its cup so that the seed is visible from the outside of the cup. Have each group observe its seed for a week, comparing the seed's growth to the information shared below. Conclude the activity by having the class compare the rates at which the various fruit seeds grew.

How Seeds Grow Into Trees

A seed contains parts that develop into the trunk and roots of a tree. After a seed separates from its parent tree, it rests for a while on the ground. Water, air, and sunlight help the seed begin to grow, or *germinate.* The part of the seed that develops into the trunk points upward toward the sunlight. As the seed absorbs water, the root parts swell and burst through the seed's shell. The root grows, pushing down into the soil. As the root soaks up water from the soil, the trunk begins to develop leaves.

Truly "Tree-rrific" Trees!

Arbor Day celebrates the importance of trees in our lives. Read the topics below. Then research five facts about each one. Afterward use the facts to write a poem about trees. Use the words in your poem to form the shape of a treetop for the tree trunk pictured below.

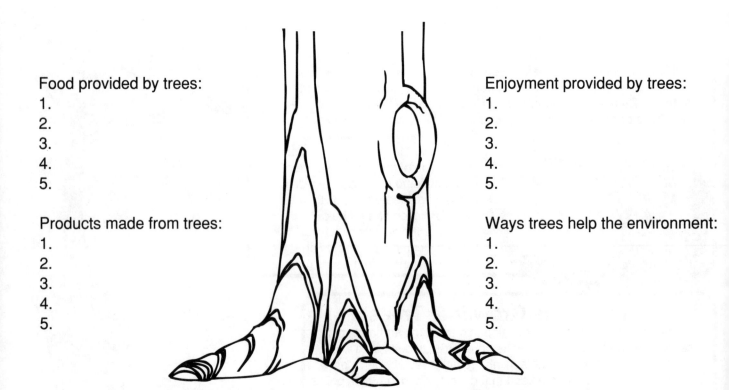

Food provided by trees:
1.
2.
3.
4.
5.

Products made from trees:
1.
2.
3.
4.
5.

Enjoyment provided by trees:
1.
2.
3.
4.
5.

Ways trees help the environment:
1.
2.
3.
4.
5.

Note To The Teacher: Provide each student with a copy of this page, appropriate reference materials, scissors, and crayons or colored pencils. After each student writes her poem, have her color it and cut it out. Post the poems on a display titled "Truly 'Tree-rrific' Trees!"

Arbor Day: research, creating a comic strip

Is There A Doctor In The Forest?

Throughout a tree's lifetime, many things may threaten its health, such as diseases, pests, and pollution. Follow the directions below to investigate some of the problems faced by trees.

Directions:

1. Research five problems that threaten a tree's health.
2. In each blank comic-strip box below, illustrate a different problem.
3. Write a sentence in each box to accompany the illustration.
4. Color and cut out your comic strip to share with the class.

Oh, Doctor, I have so many problems!

Bonus Box: Choose one of the problems shown in your comic strip. Then, on the back of this sheet, write a prescription that will help the tree remedy its problem.

Note To The Teacher: Provide each student with appropriate reference materials, crayons or colored pencils, scissors, glue, and a 9" x 12" sheet of colored construction paper. After the student has cut out his comic strip, direct him to glue the strip to the construction-paper sheet and title it. Post the comic strips in a display titled "Is There A Doctor In The Forest?"

Planting A Forest And Watching It Grow

Imagine that you are part of a special forestry research team. Research the answers to the activities below. After you complete each activity, color the tree beside it. Your team then earns a tree to "plant" in its forest. See how many trees your team can "plant" before Arbor Day. It just may inspire you to plant a real tree and watch it grow!

 1. Trees are grouped into two main categories: *evergreen* and *deciduous*. Make a chart showing the differences between the two types. Be sure to give an example for each one.

 2. Some trees grow to be very tall—taller than 30-story buildings! Record the name of the tallest tree in the world and its average height.

 3. You can tell how old a person is by asking him how many birthdays he has celebrated. Draw a picture that shows how to tell the age of a tree.

 4. Trees are the oldest known living things. Describe two of the oldest trees in the world. Tell where they are located and their approximate ages.

 5. Almost every state has a *forester* whose job is to protect the state's forests. Write a newspaper advertisement for a state forester that explains what you think this job involves.

 6. The *gypsy moth, tussock moth,* and *spruce budworm* all have something in common. Write a sentence explaining what these insects do to trees.

 7. There are thousands of kinds of trees. List five states and a tree that grows in each one.

 8. Each year, *loggers* cut down millions of trees in the world's forests. These trees are used to create many types of products. List ten products made from trees.

 9. People throughout the world eat food provided by trees. Research foods that come from trees; then list your five favorites.

 10. Trees need lots of water! Solve the following problems:
- If a large apple tree uses 95 gallons of water from the soil in one day, how many gallons of water is that in one week? In one month?
- On a hot summer day, some trees move water up their trunks at a rate of 3 feet per minute. If the tree is 168 feet tall, how many minutes would it take the water to reach the top of the tree?

Answer Keys

Page 6

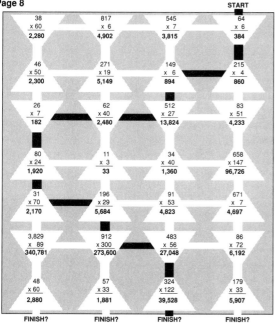

76	52	24	62	115	98	23	13	10
19	22	89	73	20	93	14	7	92
95	47	126	82	135	31	80	90	102
33	70	17	73	41	27	52	22	87
56	130	22	58	53	33	92	69	58
15	13	105	10	57	20	72	25	61
110	19	43	78	87	89	33	49	100
44	69	14	13	43	56	12	36	85
66	55	11	99	44	23	8	7	15

Page 7

Across

A. 1,155
B. 5,037
C. 6,336
D. 2,952
E. 21,966
F. 93,177
G. 5,625
H. 84,539
I. 8,835

Down

J. 15
K. 506
L. 5,332
M. 7,392
N. 651
O. 299
P. 63
Q. 615
R. 768
S. 7,248
T. 558
U. 33
V. 95

Page 8

			START
38 × 60 = 2,280	817 × 6 = 4,902	545 × 7 = 3,815	64 × 6 = 384
46 × 50 = 2,300	271 × 19 = 5,149	149 × 6 = 894	215 × 4 = 860
26 × 7 = 182	62 × 40 = 2,480	512 × 27 = 13,824	83 × 51 = 4,233
80 × 24 = 1,920	11 × 3 = 33	34 × 40 = 1,360	658 × 147 = 96,726
31 × 70 = 2,170	196 × 29 = 5,684	91 × 53 = 4,823	671 × 7 = 4,697
3,829 × 89 = 340,781	912 × 300 = 273,600	483 × 56 = 27,048	86 × 72 = 6,192
48 × 60 = 2,880	57 × 33 = 1,881	324 × 122 = 39,528	179 × 33 = 5,907
FINISH?	FINISH?	FINISH?	FINISH?

Page 9

1. 117 R1
2. 25 R4
3. 1,119 R2
4. 121 R3
5. 1,147 R1
6. 51 R5
7. 1,974 R1
8. 1,139 R3
9. 84 R5
10. 138 R5
11. 1,286 R2
12. 43 R2
13. 748 R4
14. 81 R7
15. 966 R1
16. 740 R4

Bonus Box: 50 = "Dividend Doo-wop"

Page 10

Answers may vary. Here are some possible solutions.

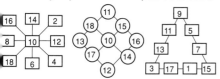

Page 11

Answers may vary. Here are some possible solutions.

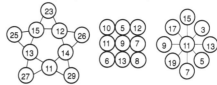

Page 12

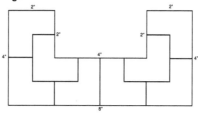

Page 15

Accept reasonable answers.

3 Use a shovel to remove the grass and other plants that cover the site.
10 Water your garden when the soil gets dry.
5 Add fertilizer after breaking up the soil.
2 Many flowers and most vegetables need a large amount of light to grow well.
4 Dig up the soil 8 to 12 inches.
9 Plant vegetables in straight rows so they can be cared for more easily.
1 Choose a site where the soil won't get soggy.
8 Space the seeds apart so the plants will have enough room to grow.
7 Choose plants that grow well in your climate.
6 Draw a sketch of your garden before planting to avoid making mistakes.

Page 34

A.

Scale	2 inches = ? miles	2 1/2 inches = ? miles	5 inches = ? miles	10 inches = ? miles
1 inch = 8 miles	16 miles	20 miles	40 miles	80 miles
1 inch = 10 miles	20 miles	25 miles	50 miles	100 miles
1 inch = 50 miles	100 miles	125 miles	250 miles	500 miles
1 inch = 100 miles	200 miles	250 miles	500 miles	1000 miles

B. (Answers may vary slightly.)
1. 2 miles
2. 11 miles
3. 7 miles
4. 14 miles
5. Jamestown
6. 2 miles

Bonus Box: Jamestown to Sky Lake = about 9 minutes
Jamestown to Copper Mountain = about 16.5 minutes
Jamestown to Marieville = about 21 minutes

Page 35

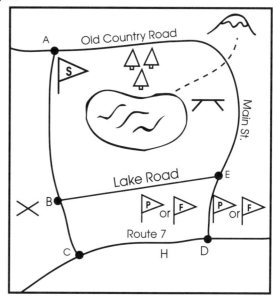

63

Answer Keys

Page 40
1. twice
2. half
3. equal
4. more than
5. same
6. total
7. three times
8. greater than
9. less than
10. in all

Page 42
1. streetcar
2. superstar
3. registrar
4. St. Bernard
5. starvation
6. sanitary
7. postmark
8. sanctuary
9. starfish
10. streamer
11. sweetheart
12. stairs
13. secretary
14. satisfactory
15. startle
16. strawberry

Page 43
1. (Stars) shine; **Agree**
2. (Cliffs and craters) scars; **Disagree**
3. (The Sun) moves; **Agree**
4. (Earth) tilts; **Agree**
5. (We) lives; **Disagree**
6. (A scientist) measure; **Disagree**
7. (The Moon's gravity) cause; **Disagree**
8. (Rusty-red rock) covers; **Agree**
9. (A huge storm cloud) rages; **Agree**
10. (Icy particles) makes; **Disagree**
11. (Uranus) orbits; **Agree**
12. (Poisonous clouds) swirl; **Agree**
13. (Pluto) spends; **Agree**

A	S	T	R	O	N	O	M	Y		I	S		A	W	E	S	O	M	E !
7	5	1	4	13	6	13	9	3		12	5		7	11	2	5	13	9	2

Page 47
Activity 1—See map.
Activity 2—See map. Descriptions will vary.
Activity 3—See map.
1. Washington
2. Oregon
3. Idaho

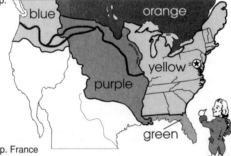

blue
orange
yellow
purple
green

Activity 4—See map. France
Activity 5—See map.
Accept any three states from the following: Montana, Wyoming, Colorado, North Dakota, South Dakota, Nebraska, Kansas, Oklahoma, Minnesota, Iowa, Missouri, Arkansas, Louisiana
Activity 6—See map.

Page 48
The Triassic Period (Accept any order.)
1. Staurikosaurus
2. Chasmatosaurus
3. Plateosaurus

The Jurassic Period (Accept any order.)
4. Stegosaurus
5. Allosaurus
6. Seismosaurus

The Cretaceous Period (Accept any order.)
7. Triceratops
8. Tyrannosaurus
9. Iguanodon
10. Pteranodon

Page 51
1. There are 42 pennies in all. 42 ÷ 3 = 14. Remove one penny from the first stack and three pennies from the third stack. Add them to the middle stack.
2. 2 quarters, 1 dime, 1 nickel
   2 quarters, 0 dimes, 3 nickels
   1 quarter, 4 dimes, 0 nickels
   1 quarter, 3 dimes, 2 nickels
   1 quarter, 2 dimes, 4 nickels
   1 quarter, 1 dime, 6 nickels
   1 quarter, 0 dimes, 8 nickels
   0 quarters, 6 dimes, 1 nickel
   0 quarters, 5 dimes, 3 nickels
   0 quarters, 4 dimes, 5 nickels
   0 quarters, 3 dimes, 7 nickels
   0 quarters, 2 dimes, 9 nickels
   0 quarters, 1 dime, 11 nickels
   0 quarters, 0 dimes, 13 nickels
3. 17 moves (The coins are represented by 1, 5, 10, 25. Make the following moves: 10-B, 1-C, 10-C, 5-B, 10-A, 1-B, 10-B, 25-C, 10-A, 1-C, 10-B, 1-A, 10-A, 5-C, 10-B, 1-C, 10-C.)

Page 52
1. pence	1. (10,8) (5,10) (1,11) (7,1) (10,4) (6,7) (7,1)
2. peso	2. (11,1) (8,3) (11,9) (6,7)
3. franc	3. (12,6) (8,3) (4,1) (8,9) (6,7) (5,5)
4. centavo	4. (2,5) (6,7) (12,6) (12,6) (4,8)
5. fils	
6. yen	
7. lira	
8. kobo	

Page 60
Accept reasonable responses. Answers for each category may include:
Food provided by trees:
1. fruits such as avocados, grapefruits, oranges, apples, etc.
2. nuts such as pecans, walnuts, and pine nuts
3. chocolate
4. coffee
5. maple syrup

Products made from trees:
1. medicines
2. fibers for textiles
3. wood for furniture and paper
4. fuel
5. rubber

Enjoyment provided by trees:
1. climbing
2. swinging
3. relaxing in their shade
4. camping
5. observing wildlife

Trees help the environment by:
1. providing shelter for many animals and insects
2. helping to conserve water
3. enriching the soil
4. keeping the wind from blowing away topsoil
5. renewing the atmosphere by removing carbon dioxide and giving off oxygen

Page 62
Accept reasonable responses.

1.

Evergreens	Deciduous
have needle-shaped leaves	have broad leaves
bear foliage all year	lose their leaves one time a year
shed small amounts of leaves, replacing them with new ones	as the cold season approaches; replace the leaves with new ones in the spring
Examples: bristlecone, cedar, cypress, Douglas-fir, sequoia, spruce	**Examples:** ash, beech, chestnut, maple

2. The tallest tree is the redwood, which can grow more than 360 feet tall.
3. Count the rings in its trunk to find the age of a tree.
4. Two of the oldest trees are the bristlecone pine and the giant sequoia. Both are found in California. Some bristlecone pines have lived between 4,000 and 5,000 years. Some sequoias are about 3,500 years old.
5. Answers will vary. A state forester is responsible for the administration and protection of state forestlands.
6. These insects destroy large areas of forest by eating all the leaves off trees.
7. Answers will vary.
8. Answers will vary. Some products include medicines, fibers for textiles, wood for furniture and tools, paper, fuel, rubber, and cork.
9. Answers will vary. Some foods include fruits, nuts, chocolate, coffee, maple syrup, olives, and spices.
10. 95 gallons in 1 day x 7 days in 1 week = 665 gallons per week; 665 gallons in 1 week x 4 weeks in 1 month = 2,660 gallons per month; 168 feet ÷ 3 feet per minute = 56 minutes